MW00987480

# THE ALCHEMY OF PRAYER

*Rekindling Our Inner Life*

## Books by Terry Lynn Taylor

*Messengers of Light: The Angels' Guide to Spiritual Growth*

*Guardians of Hope: The Angels' Guide to Personal Growth*

*Answers From the Angels: A Book of Angel Letters*

*Creating With the Angels:
An Angel-Guided Journey Into Creativity*

*The Alchemy of Prayer: Rekindling Our Inner Life*

# THE ALCHEMY OF PRAYER

## *Rekindling Our Inner Life*

Terry Lynn Taylor

**H J KRAMER INC**
**TIBURON, CALIFORNIA**

H J Kramer Inc
P.O. Box 1082
Tiburon, CA 94920

Editor: Nancy Grimley Carleton
Editorial Assistant: Claudette Charbonneau
Cover Design: Jim Marin/Marin Graphic Services
Composition: Classic Typography
Book Production: Schuettge & Carleton
Manufactured in the United States of America.
10 9 8 7 6 5 4 3 2 1

Library of Congress Cataloging-in-Publication Data
Taylor, Terry Lynn, 1955–
   The alchemy of prayer : rekindling our inner life / Terry Lynn
Taylor.
      p.   cm.
   ISBN 0-915811-70-7 (hardcover)
   1. Prayer.   I. Title.
BL560.T38   1996
291.4'3–dc20                                    95-22726
                                                CIP

*What is a saint? A saint is someone
who has achieved a remote human possibility.
It is impossible to say what that possibility is.
I think it has something to do with the energy of love.
Contact with this energy results in the exercise
of a kind of balance in the chaos of existence.
A saint does not dissolve the chaos: if he did
the world would have changed long ago.
I do not think that a saint dissolves the chaos even
for himself, for there is something arrogant and warlike
in the notion of a man setting the universe in order.
It is a kind of balance that is his glory.
He rides the drifts like an escaped ski. . . .
Something in him so loves the world that he gives himself
to the laws of gravity and change.*
—Leonard Cohen

## To Our Readers

The books we publish
are our contribution to
an emerging world based on
cooperation rather than on competition,
on affirmation of the human spirit rather
than on self-doubt, and on the certainty
that all humanity is connected.
Our goal is to touch as many
lives as possible with a
message of hope for
a better world.

*Hal and Linda Kramer, Publishers*

# CONTENTS

# Introduction:
# The Alchemical Path of Prayer

*Lead will play its role until the world
has no further need for lead;
and then lead will have to turn itself into gold.
That's what alchemists do. They show that,
when we strive to become better than we are,
everything around us becomes better, too.*

—Paulo Coelho

O n Earth, every moment of our lives brings change. Some of these changes may be joyous, while others are heart wrenching. Either way, change comes whether we seek it or not. We try to cope with change in many ways, often through bringing a semblance of order to our lives, because order offers the illusion of control. And yet we have no way of knowing the ultimate effect of the changes that life presents to us. Sometimes the most difficult changes can bring about the deepest spiritual awakenings.

When I am talking with people who have reached a level of keen awareness of an obstacle in their lives, emotional or physical, people who long for profound transformation, I often say to them, "Change the chemistry." What I mean by this is that when we reach a certain level of awareness, change will occur, and we can help this change along by knowing how to shift the chemistry—the complex of emotions, the cauldron of reactions—in a new and positive direction.

Chemistry by definition is the scientific study of substances and their elements and how they react when combined. The word *chemistry* comes from the medieval word *alchemy.* Alchemy is the art of turning base metals, such as lead, into gold, and, even more important, it is the art of knowing. Knowing is awareness, and awareness holds the power to bring true change.

The title of this book, *The Alchemy of Prayer,* came to me in an alchemical way. I was having a very difficult time knowing how to take the information I wanted to share about prayer and present it in book form. I prayed daily for guidance, but I still felt stuck. In my most frustrated moment, I mentioned my problem to my friend and spiritual sister Shannon. She asked me to tell her about what I wanted to convey in the book. So I shared some of my ideas, and she blurted out, "The alchemy of prayer," and I said, "That's it." By stirring around the concepts with

Shannon, someone who genuinely cares about me, by heating them up with my frustration, naming them, and wanting to transmute the situation, we achieved alchemy and an answer to my daily prayers.

In this book, I use the term *alchemy* to represent the actual spiritual changes that happen when we pray. Once we decide to follow our spiritual path and use our free will to love God, we truly are "born again." We are changed forever alchemically. When we make the choice to understand God and the spiritual side of ourselves, we attain an awareness of heavenly beauty that will never leave us. Even if we try to go back and live the way we once did, unconscious of heaven's love, we can't do it. We will never be the same once we begin the awakening process, yet we will always be ourselves. This is the path of spiritual alchemy. Sometimes we may not like the lessons we receive, yet oftentimes the beauty and joy will astound us.

The history of alchemy tells of the "philosopher's stone" alchemists searched for that would allow them to transmute base metals into gold. This is a powerful symbol. I believe it represents the touching of our consciousness by divine love from God and the angels. Interactions with angels create such powerful changes in people's lives because angels vibrate on a level so high that the least interchange with them raises our own vibration, changing our consciousness and repositioning us in the direction of the golden light of spiritual transformation. The philosopher's stone symbolizes the instrument for bringing about the physical and spiritual chemistry changes that happen when we are seized by divine love. Symbols are portals into the deep mysteries that surround us and weave magic through our lives. We are responsible for mining our own philosopher's stone, which symbolizes our longing to find our spiritual roots, our true nature.

The base metals of the alchemical process represent the undeveloped divine self, or the primal elements that we are born with. Since all manifest existence revolves around change, each element can potentially transform into something else. Gold is symbolic of innate purity and the ability to radiate a steady luster of spiritual light. As alchemists, we are the most important secret ingredient in the process of alchemy. We face the challenge of cultivating the climate in ourselves to attract and make use of the invisible divine spark that brings about the desired transformation.

## Becoming "Prayer Aware"

A prayer is an expression of thoughts, hopes, or needs directed to a deity, or Higher Power; it can be an earnest appeal, a solemn request, or a gesture of thanksgiving. Prayer is an important component in all religious traditions. Although prayer may take on different forms, its essence is always the same.

Prayer has been receiving more attention recently, and tremendous potential lies in this renewed interest. Combine this resurgence with the fact that angel consciousness is reawakening, and we are blessed with the ingredients to create a truly positive transformation on our planet. I am filled with deep joy when I realize how many people are turning to prayer for the first time in their lives, or are returning to prayer after a long absence.

Recently a major magazine published an article about prayer that included some quotes from prominent authors saying that prayer can be misused in a way they labeled "narcissistic" and "manipulative." They were concerned that people would pray for things they wanted, or pray "just because it works." While I am glad that prayer is a popular subject, I am not glad to see articles that might discourage some people from praying because they fear they aren't "doing it right," or, worse, because they fear that they'll be labeled "narcissists" if they ask the Great Creator for something specific. Narcissism is a seriously pathological condition; it is extremely difficult to treat, and fortunately it is not as common as we are led to believe.

Can you imagine a group of "prayer police" running around stopping people in the middle of their prayers and saying, "Excuse me, but you can't ask for anything in your prayers," or "You are kneeling the wrong way"? I simply can't imagine stopping others and telling them that they are not praying right!

Personally, I think the best authority on prayer is our inner guidance and our awareness that when we pray, God is the force listening. When we ask God for anything in prayer, whether our request is "narcissistic" or not, God remains the same, and we will receive what we need *spiritually,* that is, whatever is spiritually appropriate for our personal situation. Each of us has our own special relationship with God, so our prayers will be an expression of that relationship. Keep in mind that others do not need to know what you pray for or how you pray, unless you want them to. Begin to trust your own inner authority.

Because some reports have shown that prayer makes a difference in physical healing and in predicted outcomes for certain situations, some scientists have wanted to conduct studies to figure out whether this is true and how and why it happens. I say let them have their fun! But the truth is that we don't really need to know exactly why prayer works; our soul already knows that it does. Our spirit guides us in prayer, and our logical mind is often left confused, but we are more than our mind. We feel, hear, and record much more information than we realize, and we are guided by a higher frame of reference that knows things in the space beyond linear time.

You might look back on the times in your life when you thought you were steering the ship, when you thought you were really in charge. Consider all that unfolded to get you where you are now. Perhaps you will become aware that there was also a mysterious force at work. As soon as we make prayer an everyday part of our lives, we will steer ourselves toward wisdom, put our light on the map that shows our unfolding path, and attract God by allowing the beauty of our soul to reflect God's light.

### About the Book

My goal in writing books is to offer information that I feel the angels want us to know. You may wonder how *I*, Terry Lynn Taylor, would know what the angels want us to know. Well, it is by no magical trick! It is by studying spiritual law and by noticing how my heart responds when I meditate on, pray about, and contemplate the angels. In blessed moments, I receive a sense of knowing that I would never ruin with an "ex-planation." I am tired of people trying to flatten everything out so they can see ahead. My favorite view is the one with peaks and valleys to climb and explore. I don't want a flat life; I don't need everything to be explained. I want to learn about life with the angels, and by choosing this path, I know I accept all of the ups and downs, the bright colors, the dark nights, the tears and the laughter.

I believe that the angels want us to know how to include prayer in our lives. The goal of a spiritual life is integration and wholeness. Prayer leads us to this point, because it doesn't simply work on the outer planes but starts to change us from within. The truth lives within us; its light shines from our core, from our heart. When we begin to feel comfortable with the inner dimensions of our being, then we will begin to feel truly whole. The journey within takes time, patience, hope, gratitude, and a personal understanding of the Great Creator. After we have gone within and transformed our own lead to gold, we will naturally come out into the light and share our love with the world while holding the pure intention in our hearts of helping God and the angels transform the lead of the world's sorrow into hope and right living.

# PART ONE

## TEMPLE OF PRAYER

### *On Earth as It Is in Heaven*

*We are a holy temple,*
*Made of both Earth and sky.*
*In this temple, we voice our prayer*
*And God hears, and knows our heart.*
*Prayer allows us a direct awareness of God.*
*Our devotion expresses great love, and*
*When we allow love for the Creator*
*To flow out from us,*
*Our lives naturally unfold*
*In a heavenly direction.*
*Even when we feel lost,*
*We are found by the angels.*
*The angels remind us who we are.*

# The Alchemy of Prayer

## *Awakening Our Voice*

*The Alchemists knew their work of transmuting
the lead of ignorance and separation
into the gold of union would best be done
gently, patiently, and with great delicacy.
As the windows of the heart are opened,
the light pours in, revealing what was
previously shrouded in darkness.
Insight, wisdom, compassion grow with
the experience of communion with the Divine.*
— Anne Baring and Andrew Harvey

*I* would love to start out this discussion with a perfect definition of prayer, one that would make so much sense to all who read it that they would immediately put the book down and begin to pray. I won't be able to do that because prayer is so personal and resides in the non-rational realm. Prayer is a subject that seems problematic for some people. People who don't pray get very nervous when I ask them about prayer; they probably think that prayer relates exclusively to religion. There are also people who fear prayer because they fear God.

One reason it is difficult for me to define prayer is because I was taught to pray at a very young age, and I don't remember how it was presented to me. At that young age, I remember knowing that God was everywhere, and I would talk to God the same way I would talk to a tree or a rosebush. I remember times when I felt so much love wash over me from God that my heart took up the entire backyard. It seemed to me then, and now, that prayer is a natural part of life, just as natural as our ability to walk, talk, and think.

Here are some of my inner knowings about prayer:

• To pray means to communicate with the very heart and soul of our Universe.

• Prayer offers a way to tap into the source of pure love.

• Prayer is spiritual fuel; it is light; and it guides us to understand the Universal Consciousness.

• Prayer offers a renewal of faith, inspiration, and meaning.

• Prayer is an offering of love that engages our highest beingness.

- Prayer allows us to listen to the voice within, to our deepest honesty.
- Prayer gives us the chance to step aside from our seat of control and witness Divine Providence in action.

I like to think of prayer as the way we place ourselves and our path on the spiritual map. Imagine that each person who prays is like a light on the Earth, shining like a bright star in the night. Light attracts light, so by praying and putting ourselves on the spiritual map, we are attracting God in the sweetest way. You possess a compass within your soul that always points you to your destiny and to God. Prayer is one of the ways you can get in touch with the messages of your soul, for when you pray, you speak your deepest truth.

Praying is making "a sound unto the Lord," but it does not necessarily mean we make a vocal noise. It means that we send out a vibration of our inner light by means of our "prayer voice." This voice is a part of all of us, even if we haven't yet acknowledged it. For people who have been praying for most of their lives, this voice is a familiar part of themselves. Take time to know the voice in you that prays and connects your light to the divine source. Let it have its say; let it find a home in your consciousness. Let it emerge gently, and try not to direct it. Allow it time to unfold in grace. Ask the angels to help you know this voice that comes from the depths of your being, from the seeds of light in your soul.

Praying is often a silent activity, although prayers can also be sung, cried out loud, spoken, or said together with a group. Prayers can be written as declarations, poems, or requests. Prayers can be visualized, made into art, or acted out in a ritual. There are many ways to pray, and there are many reasons to pray. Prayer can be a serious, solemn event, a time to be with pain and allow transformation. Yet you are also free to have fun with prayer, especially with the angels as prayer partners. As humans, we have a range of possible experiences, and prayer is a time to honor whatever we are feeling.

Prayer is a vital part of an imaginative, creative, and heart-centered life. Prayer affects us deeply, and knowing this opens up a new door in our imagination. The most interesting thing about prayer is that it is very practical. Prayer is actually therapy. When you pray, you are engaging in a psychic process of healing, and exercising the skill to solve problems with your inner wisdom. You are also programming your mind to look for positive solutions and to calm down and *respond* wisely to life instead of over-reacting to situations.

What is the highest and best way to pray? If I were to answer this, I would be acting as an authority on prayer, and I am not one. I am simply someone who has always understood how important prayer is and how ultimately loving God is. I can say that the more often we pray, the less we grovel or beg for things. Oftentimes we start out praying as if we were children pleading with a parent. We then come to a point where we recognize that we are co-creators of our lives, and we become active players in our prayer outcomes

So why take the time to pray? At the deepest level, we don't really need to know *why* we pray, because the reasons are multidimensional and mutable as our situation changes. It is best to make prayer a part of your life without having to analyze it, or know too much about the mechanics. Let prayer be a truthful, spontaneous response to life. No matter how you feel, just be real with God and communicate from that space. As Matthew Fox says in his book about prayer, *On Becoming a Musical Mystical Bear,* "A response is spontaneous (from the Latin *sponte,* of one's own will): it is free, it is mine. We respond *because we feel like it* . . . it is simply an utterance of one's deep feelings." By responding to God, we instantly change the chemistry of any situation to a higher vibration, regardless of the whys and hows.

When we pray, we are seeking divine wisdom, regardless of what our words or intentions may indicate. Wisdom is not easy to define, and it is not easy to find pure examples of wisdom in contemporary life. If we go looking for wisdom in all the usual places — TV, politics, group mentality, leaders, popular culture — we will probably find a lack of wisdom rather than truly good examples. So what constitutes wisdom? I think there are some definite indicators. For one, I always sense wisdom in people who can admit that they were wrong, or who can say that their thoughts and beliefs have changed. I am repelled, however, when I see people hanging on and defending worn-out beliefs just because they are afraid they may look foolish if they admit the need for a change. The wise are not concerned with appearances or with what others may think; they act on their truth. It takes a lot of wisdom to be a fool, to travel the fool's journey. Wisdom is admitting that we really don't know, and only by this admission will we begin to know.

Prayer has true transformative power. As I stated in the Introduction, prayer changes the chemistry of a situation. By connecting with God on a regular basis, we are always in the process of turning our lead into gold. Before we even begin the action of praying, God and the angels know what we need. When we are living in accordance with Divine Providence, prayer becomes so integrated into our waking life that we don't even need to pray consciously; our life has become our prayer. One of the best ways to sprinkle gold dust on our goals and dreams is to pray for divine inspiration and faith to lead us to the truth, not necessarily for the goals themselves. In other words, God knows what our goals are, and often we short-change ourselves when we fixate too much on specifics. For when we are filled with divine inspiration, we have all that we need to live magnificent lives.

## Prayer Basics

### *Where to Pray*

• Pray anywhere and everywhere. Pray on your own or with others. Pray in your home, in your car, in a park, or in a church, but most of all, pray in the temple of your own mind.

### *When to Pray*

• Pray all the time; make your life a prayer. Pray consciously to change a situation, pray when you feel intense fear, pray when you feel joy and thanksgiving, pray when you fear for others, pray when you know you need a change in your life, and pray as a response to life.

### *How to Pray*

• Begin praying, and you will come to know the best way to pray for you. Your form of praying may vary from day to day. There are as many ways to pray as there are individuals. Just let yourself begin.

# The Alchemy of Devotion to God

## *"Thy Will Be Done"*

*It is not enough to do good things*
*and then you'll be a good person.*
*It's knowing that your goodness*
*is a manifestation of God.*

— Thomas Merton

*I* always address God, the Highest Light in the Universe, the Creator, the Great Spirit, when I pray. The most important truth in prayer is that we are communicating with the highest, most powerful energy in the universe. It doesn't matter to me if you believe that God is a leaf on a tree or the brightest star in the night; I will respect and honor your belief. I will try to be careful not to overdefine God in this book. Mostly, I hope to present ideas that can help you build your own strong spiritual foundation of prayer and perhaps strengthen your relationship with God, the Universe, the Great Creator.

When I use the word *God,* I hope you'll understand it in this way: Just as "the one moon shows in every pool; in every pool, the one moon," the one God—the ultimate source of divine love and energy—shines in every heart of every person regardless of race, religion, location, or station in life. Divine light doesn't change with different names or rituals; the light is the light is the light. Does the sun change when sunlight falls upon different faces? The sun remains the same regardless. We are the receivers of the light, and we each have our own ways of facing the light.

There is no power greater than God. As the Bible states: "In the beginning was the Word, and the Word was with God, and the Word was God." The Word is sound—the vibration from which all things are created, the divine mantra. Sound is the womb of the Divine Mother, the Earth. Take a moment and think about the idea that we come from a vibration, from a divine sound. Close your eyes and listen for the sound of God. As you renew yourself with the harmonious tones of the Universe, begin to find God within you. Where is your connecting point to this harmonious vibration? Your heart? Your mind? This will be personal to you. You may feel God in your heart, or you may experience God as a field of energy encompassing you—the God within. When we allow God's energy to play within our being, we establish alignment with our spiritual center.

Now let us shift gears and consider God the infinite —
God who is above, the transcendent force, the beauty of
which inspires us to cry out to the sky and sing praises
with the angels. Think about the expansiveness of the
Universe. Think about the magnificent force of beauty
when the clouds join the setting sun in a symphony of
color. Imagine yourself on the highest mountaintop over-
looking a sea of humanity. Feel the aching in your heart
to fly with the angels out into the ethers, up through the
majestic clouds. Begin to experience the idea of God as
the Universe — the perfect Universe, which provides exactly what we need and gifts us with unlimited possibilities
to create and to be love.

The center inside yourself where you experience God
may change when you are in various mental spaces. For
example, when you are feeling like a tiny drop in the
ocean, in awe of how small a human life can seem, then
you may want to cry out to God the expansive and ask
that God bring the energy within you to remind you that
no matter how many humans there are on planet Earth,
each individual life is an incredible miracle of great
importance. Each of us has a guardian angel, and our
angel whispers in our ear, reminding us to pay loving
attention to God. This keeps us moving toward God, and
leads us to a sense of completeness within ourselves.
When we pay attention to God, our life has profound

purpose and meaning. We are given a ticket to a deep experience of the divine wherever we go.

In the Bible it is written that "with God all things are possible." The archangel Gabriel told this to Mary when she could not believe that she could conceive a son with the Holy Spirit. "For with God nothing is ever impossible, *and* no word from God shall be without power *or* impossible of fulfillment" (Luke 1:37, Amplified Bible). We are part of these infinite possibilities, and the choices we make create the big picture. We can choose to create many wonderful miracles that will make the world better, and give us grace beyond comparison. But because *all* things are possible, this means that we can also make choices to ruin things.

Success comes from creating what we want in life without compromising our values or the balance of natural laws. At our deepest core, we know these laws, but sometimes we resist them. This book does not recount basic spiritual laws, but rather aims to help you align yourself with the laws naturally, through prayer and knowing God in your own way. We have so much help available to us. We have angels to guide us, and we have a sense of humor. Prayer is essential to our spiritual life. It is not just the act of praying that is essential—that can be too automatic—but the art of communicating with life, with the divine, so that you are building a strong foundation for your spirit to soar.

Your heart knows that with God all things are possible. Instead of trying to believe this and intellectualize the possibilities, just allow yourself to know it deeply. Let your knowing run like a fresh mountain stream, bubbling up from the source, always moving. Remind yourself daily. There are various ways to think about this powerful idea: that with God all things are possible. At times when you pray to God and find that your faith seems to be wavering, just remember that God knows the language of your heart. Our mind, our intellect, and what we see with our eyes are but tiny fractions of what surrounds us. Sometimes when we pray for help, we begin by doing battle with our intellectual mind, which wants to know all the hows and whys. Faith comes with practice and by knowing that the imagination of God lies far beyond anything that our mind can perceive or control.

Often when we are stuck in the throes of a dilemma, such as our pain, we forget that everything in life can change in an instant. I probably do not need to remind you how fragile human life is. Know God now, while you are here. Understand that you are free to have your own special relationship with the divine. You weren't sent to Earth with all the rules clearly defined, all the answers laid out, or all of the steps ahead of you laid out in linear order. You were sent to Earth with definite gifts and abilities, the most important one being your ability to receive and share love. Remember that you are a possibility of God, and you entertain God when you "follow your bliss" and free your spirit to be true to yourself.

Know that in the wide range of human experiences and emotions, God sometimes feels very much within us and at other times seems out beyond our reach. No matter—God is always there and present for us to send our prayers to. Having a foundation made of God means that when we fall down, when we hit the bottom, we will fall into the arms of God. If the foundation of our life is spiritual, we walk on the temple floor in our daily life. Now, if we don't have God as our foundation, when we fall we may land in the swamp waters of the wasteland. In these waters, people either drown or surrender at last to God. The Buddhists like to use the analogy of the lotus forming itself into perfection from the sludge and murk of a pond. This is pure alchemy: sludge being transformed into beauty. We are never lost, but often we must take action to be found.

In the Bible is the powerful statement "Thy will be done, on Earth as it is in the heavens." The word *will* is defined as "the mental faculty by which one deliberately chooses or decides upon a course of action, volition; choice; strong purpose; determination." We use the word *will* often, and most of us have heard that as humans we possess free will. Having free will means that we are free to make choices. We are given free will so that it will be our own choice to love God and do God's will on Earth. When you choose to live your life for the good of the divine, you have given God a great gift of love.

The first true spiritual awakening any one of us can have is to *freely* choose to use our precious life for the glory of the divine. The next step is to bring ourselves in alignment with the will of God, which is really very simple. The point that most people miss is that we do this out of love and gratitude, *not out of suffering or fear,* and no one is forcing us to choose to do God's will. When you choose to live your life spiritually out of a deep love for God, then you naturally come into alignment with your soul, your spirit, your gifts, and your life's purpose. Difficulties arise when we lose devotion, and devotion entails great love. If you are living a spiritual life and you rarely have moments of great love for the Creator, something essential is missing. It is nearly impossible to devote yourself to something or someone without great love in your heart.

Living a life of devotion and doing God's will means that we have to be creative. To be truly creative, we must be inspired, for when we are inspired, we find our own unique way to know and love God. This is all very simple, but not very easy. That is why some people choose to become devotees of a guru, so that they can learn how to stay on the path of devotion. We can choose to be like the angels and devote ourselves directly to God, but this requires action on our part. We cannot sit around letting the days pass just because we think that everything is God's will, so why act upon anything. Part of our mission is to pray, which establishes communication with God.

"Thy will be done" does not mean we get out of making difficult decisions. We still must live our lives and work through our issues. Always remember that we don't have to make our lives miserable to love God. And if we are miserable being spiritual, we are forgetting to love and to take ourselves lightly. When we allow love to energize our life, we develop passion and a deep connection to living here on Earth.

In our great love and devotion to God, it is important that we not get caught up in the ways of the world, and become too bothered by the humans who do not choose to love God. Some people seem to separate their spiritual life from their "everyday" life. Other people think that being spiritual means that they have to proselytize and try to change others' lives when they are changing their own. We do best to concentrate on our own inner work, developing God within us and not going after the devil in others. We can honor the face of God in each soul we meet. We can honor the divinity within each person, even those whom we have trouble loving. Basically, God's will will be done, because there is no power greater. Our task is to choose freely to stay awake and help God. This way, the decisions made universally are helped by the people who love God.

When we pray and ask that we want something to be done for the "highest good of all," this really means that we will accept and allow the will of God to be done. We won't try to define the outcome, and even if we don't understand it, we accept it. Humans change so much as they grow that it doesn't make sense to do things according to what *we* may think the highest good is at any moment. The point is to understand exactly what asking for the highest good means.

### Engaging in Devotional Prayer

• Prayer is the best ritualistic way to show our devotion. Devotion—great love—requires action. Pick one of the prayers in the final chapter, "The Alchemy of Our Ancestors," or any other prayer from a favorite source that speaks to your heart, and say it each morning as part of your devotion to the Great Creator, who is love supreme.

• A sweet way to show your devotion to God is to talk to God as if God is your dearest friend. Tell God all of your fears, your hopes, and your dreams, and how you feel about life each day or each hour. Be a child once in a while; it is good for you. Form a running dialogue with God. God is never far away, and when we allow the child in us to converse with God, it helps to put many things into a different perspective, which in turn creates the possibility for alchemy.

• When Jesus was asked which was the greatest of all the commandments in scriptural law, he answered, "You shall love the Lord your God with all your heart, and with all your soul, and with all your mind. The second is like it, 'You shall love your neighbor as yourself'" (Matthew 22:37, 39). Each day, put these greatest of commandments into practice in some small way.

# The Alchemy of Angels

## *Heavenly Direction*

*How wonderful it is that
nobody need wait a single moment
before starting to improve the world.*

—Anne Frank

Sometimes we get lost and refuse to ask for directions. We all know how continuing to go in the wrong direction can make things worse. When we are feeling lost in life, we have the angels on hand to help point us in the right direction. The key is that we need to stop and ask. There is no need to judge ourselves for getting lost. In fact, getting lost can be quite important at times. Getting lost might allow us to find true humility for the first time; it might help us to become conscious of the ways of angels. It is written: "For He will give His angels charge concerning you, To guard you in all your ways" (Psalm 91:11). We always receive spiritual help when we need it, want it, and ask for it through prayer.

The angels are natural prayer partners. They love our prayers. Praying makes the angels a true part of our spiritual path, for they hear our prayers and know what we are asking from God. One important point to remember is that we don't pray *to* angels, yet we can pray *with* angels. Angels are truly "messengers of God," and they can give wings to our prayers as they carry our prayers to God, to the infinite realm where all things are possible. Angels are often the answer to our prayers. A good way to address your angel, if you haven't yet received a particular name, is as "Guardian Dear."

Angels are important to prayer. Whether we are conscious of it or not, they are constantly working for God in ministering to the needs of the prayerful. Regardless of how minor the request may seem to us, it is important in heaven. However, to be fulfilled, the request has to have a spiritually attuned intent, meaning it must vibrate with what heaven has to offer. If we pray for things of the world or for ways to manipulate others, the angels can't vibrate at such a low frequency, and we will not get their assistance. Requests with low, manipulative, and selfish intentions are not truly prayers.

To have the angels in our lives, we must welcome them by cultivating and practicing the things that angels vibrate in harmony with. To allow the angels to dance in our consciousness, we must provide a dance floor that they can express themselves on. The angels vibrate at a very high frequency, and they simply can't help further any vibration of a low nature, such as greed. Beauty, prayer, gracious offerings, and simplicity, when practiced with a loving heart, allow us direct co-creative energy with the angels. Once we pass the phase of amazement regarding angels and their awesome powers, we can progress to the ultimate stage of angel consciousness, where we make the choice to use our free will and gift of life to love God and help the angels bring forth and preserve the beautiful qualities of life.

Angels have been in the news a great deal recently, and much focus has been directed toward astonishing circumstances surrounding people's experiences with angels. Angelologist K. Martin-Kuri, states: "An inherent part of working with angels is that one agrees to change all the time. These individual transformations by angels are far more powerful than those preventing-the-car-crash interventions that get all the press." In our hearts, we know that miracles happen, and that other unseen worlds exist. We do not need to be convinced that there are angels. We do not need "proof," such as "incredible" accounts of angels stopping trains or saving people from dangerous skids, to help us believe in them. Of course an angel can stop a train, or get a car out of a skid, if that is God's will, because with God all things are possible—*all things*—and the angels are extensions of God. We only need to *know* that the angels are always with us, that in our hearts we know so many things that are not to be explained, only witnessed and experienced. For many of us, the experience of angels is subtle, not dramatic, and all we need to do is calm our souls, refine our spirits, and trust they are with us.

A theory is something we use to help us understand phenomena. Theories don't need to be "proven" beyond all reasonable doubt to be useful; we can use theories simply as a way to study and think. Often in this book, I will share one of my "theories" with you, and I hope that you will experiment with including it in your own theory or discarding it as not part of your theory if you find it doesn't fit for you. One theory I like to consider is that when we vibrate at a high enough frequency, and radiate enough light and love, then we become invisible, practically speaking, to other forms of life that are vibrating at a lower rate. Angels vibrate on a frequency of divine love, which is the highest vibration in the Universe, the highest light wave out there. This is why we don't readily see angels with our eyes; they are vibrating above the physical spectrum of light. God is the ultimate source for all light and love. We cannot drain this infinite source, and when we take from divine love, more love is created for all concerned. When we choose to be vibrant with love, we replenish and energize the world around us with light.

Trusting God and the angels is not always the easiest thing for us to do. There is an ancient story about Moses and a power called the Green One that illustrates this: Moses meets the Green One in the desert, and they begin to travel together. The Green One tells Moses that he has some deeds to do, and he fears Moses will not be able to witness these deeds without judging them with indignation. He tells Moses that if he cannot trust him without judgment, he will have to leave. Moses agrees to trust him and not to judge, since he senses that he is in the presence of a great teacher and does not want the Green One to leave. As they continue their travels, eventually they come upon a fishing village, where the Green One begins to sink all the fishing boats of the villagers. Moses is quite upset by this, but he remembers his agreement not to judge and says nothing. Next they arrive at the decaying house of two devoted young men who live just outside the wall of a city of nonbelievers. The Green One goes up to the wall, which is falling down, and repairs it, but he ignores the house of the two believers. Again Moses is disturbed and confused, but he keeps quiet as he had agreed. They continue traveling together, and the Green One continues to do things that upset Moses. Finally, Moses sees something so intolerable that he can no longer hold back from making a comment and judging the situation. The Green One must now leave him, but before he goes he tells

Moses why he acted as he did. With regard to the fishing boats he sank, the Green One tells Moses that he knew that pirates were on the way to steal the boats, and by sinking them the Green One actually saved the boats from being stolen. As for the two believers, the reason the Green One fixed the wall of the city of nonbelievers was to save the two believers from ruin; their entire fortune was buried under the city wall and was about to be revealed and stolen. As the Green One left, Moses realized that all he had judged as bad and intolerable was in fact loving and compassionate.

I think this story describes our walk with the angels. To walk with the angels, we must be awake and aware. This means we witness many things we just can't believe God would allow. God doesn't always explain them to us the way the Green One did, so we have to keep trusting at times when we are about to lose faith. This also brings us many interesting and difficult questions. Are we ever supposed to stop a bad situation? When we put things into perspective and come from a prayerful place, I believe we can know when we are meant to intervene. For example, if you find yourself in a situation where someone is being physically harmed in front of you, and you are able to stop it or call for help, I'm sure you would do so, and the Green One would still be with you. The story of Moses and the Green One is meant to illustrate how often we second-guess God and the angels, labeling situations bad before we know the whole picture. Since the whole picture may not be explained to us before we leave our physical body, we need trust and faith to keep going. We achieve a state of trust and faith most easily through consistent prayer.

The angels do so much for us that we are not always aware of. Our part of the bargain is to appreciate this and cultivate gratitude, even for the things we cannot see that the angels do for us. We can show our thanks in many creative ways. We can always make our prayers into an action or a ritual. Angelologist K. Martin-Kuri suggests: "Put some flowers in your house as a love-link, or listen to a beautiful piece of music. Every time you see or hear something beautiful, consciously give it to your angels to distribute. You can translate an experience into energy which can then go into the care of your angel and be used."

### Prayer Ideas for Angel Consciousness

• Practice saying this prayer to God at night before you go to sleep:

*Dear God,*

*Give me the inner strength to change all the time and transform when needed so that I can be a strong force of love on this planet.*

*Thank you for the angels who are always with me. Please guide me through my experiences so that I will better know how to raise my own vibration to be more in tune with the angels.*

*Please help me not to judge or "jump to interpretation" when I see things in life I do not understand, including my own pain.*

*Thank you for the peace that is always available in my heart. Thank you for the awareness that, with the angels, miracles happen on a daily basis, because with you, Lord, all things are possible.*

• Create a similar prayer of your own, including God and God's messengers, the angels.

# PART TWO

# GRACE

### *The Kiss of God's Love*

*The angels sing to us sweetly of gratitude,*
*Reminding us of our greatest gift.*
*A grateful heart delivers us to grace,*
*So we meet our fate without fear.*
*When we know and trust*
*The bigger picture,*
*When we remember God and the angels,*
*We come from the ground of true humility.*
*Grace, fate, and humility*
*Are the holy waters*
*That forever nourish our soul.*

# The Alchemy of Gratitude

## *Thanking God*

*Gratitude for the abundant richness of life,*
*even in trying and troubling times,*
*is the essential link of communication with God.*
—Joe Kelly Jackson

So far along the alchemical path of prayer, we have discussed prayer, using prayer as a devotion to God, and acknowledging that God has legions of spiritual helpers—the angels—to help guide us in all our ways on Earth. The angels make our prayers possible. They are constantly working with God, and when we pray we allow the highest good to come about with the angels' help. Prayers of thanksgiving unlock the first alchemical door to grace. Through grace, we understand our fate and our destiny, and come to know that with prayer we can gain a deep understanding of our life's special path. To be true alchemists, we must know the sacred power of humility. We start with knowing, feeling, and practicing gratitude.

The word *grateful* comes from the Latin word *gratus*, which means pleasing and thankful. Also from this Latin word, we get the words *congratulate, grace, gratuity, gratify,* and *gratis.* What does being grateful really mean? We know that it means appreciating something, being pleased by an event, or realizing that we have received something freely—gratis. The word *appreciate* means to estimate the quality or value of something, to value highly, and to increase in value or price, to cherish, prize, and treasure. How much do you appreciate yourself and this gift of life? Do you ever have moments of overwhelming gratitude for the priceless and free grace of God's love?

Take a moment to stop reading and begin to be thankful for all the wonderful things around you. Make this moment of appreciation into a prayer, and as you thank the Great Creator for each thing, consciously love what you are grateful for. If you have been unaccustomed to noticing the good in your life, you may find you have to start out slow; don't worry if this process seems difficult. One of the most powerful tools of spiritual alchemy is changing your attitude to one of gratitude. Sometimes when I want to change the chemistry of my mind-set to get into the space to write, I begin a prayer by thanking God for everything I see around me. I thank God for the clothes I am wearing, for the books scattered around me, for the beauty of the color rays I am surrounded with, for the sustenance that gives me energy, and for my body, which allows me to experience the physical dimension of life. Then I begin to thank God for all the frustrations and obstacles I perceive, the troubles and the attachments in my life; I do this because I know that these are great teachers that will eventually bring me a lighter view of life.

The alchemy of gratitude happens when we begin to truly appreciate the gift of life. When we can embrace the full experience of being a human on God's green Earth, gratitude will be our prayerful response. The Tibetan Buddhists believe that a human life is a hard-won chance to evolve and learn the right way to live. If a human lifetime is thoughtlessly wasted in mere survival activities, the chance to move toward enlightenment in the future will be farther out of reach. The Buddha said, "Once the human lifetime has been lost, it will be as hard to find another as it is for an old blind turtle in the great ocean who surfaces every hundred years to come up by chance with his neck through the single golden yoke that floats randomly around in the vast ocean."

Practicing the art of alchemical gratitude means that we *consciously* choose to love. Things that we love consciously flourish. When we actively love children, they feel worthy and nurtured, and they thrive. When we love where we live, we will treat it well and it will become magnificent regardless of circumstances. Plants and pets thrive when we love them. Love makes us grow strong, rooted in Divine Light. We can incorporate this practice in any area of our lives. For instance, if you want your hair to grow strong and healthy, start to love it and be grateful for it; then give a prayer of thanks. Consciously love your body, and you will experience extra beauty shining from within. If you love your gift of life, your time spent here will be used wisely, and you will become a vision of divinity.

With all this love comes a natural response of gratitude. After we love, we give thanks to God and to the angels. The words "Thank you, God" can become a powerful prayer when they come from your heart. These words can be a mantra you use all day long. The prayer "Thank you, God" will attract the miraculous the way nothing else can, simply because you will be in the position — the conscious mind-set — to recognize the miraculous. If you have trouble with gratitude, don't be hard on yourself, and don't forget to ask for help from the angels. Gratitude radiates a highly refined vibration that reaches right up to the vibration of the angels. When you seek this vibration, your seeking alerts the angels, and they will begin helping you change your heart.

Our hearts expand when we are grateful and show it. Gratitude is something that accumulates power the more we practice it. It forms the basis for spiritual alchemy, for when our hearts lead us to a response of gratitude, this can change the very chemistry of our minds almost instantly. It is said that joy is born out of pain. To transmute the pain into joy, we need gratitude to be alive in our heart. Gratitude can also alchemically change worry. When you are worried about something, hand it over to God with thanksgiving. "Be anxious for nothing, but in everything by prayer and supplication with thanksgiving let your requests be made known to God" (Philippians 4:6).

### Ways to Practice Creative Gratitude

• Years ago, my friend Shannon used to put on classical music and sing the words "Thank you, God" to the music. She got me doing this, too, and every now and then when I hear beautiful music, these words come strongly into my mind and fill my heart with joy. Give it a try!

• Make a little gratitude box, or journal, and write down what you are thankful for each day. When there are things you are not grateful for, thank God for them anyway, with the conscious intention of changing the chemistry. Later, you might want to go back and write about what happened. Then read periodically about your gratitude transformations.

• Celebrate "Thanksgiving" once a month. Have a feast, and during the day call up all your loved ones and thank them for being in your life. My friend Kleo called me on this last Thanksgiving to thank me for being in her life, and this loving gesture created a very special chemistry that is available to us as often as we choose to create it.

• Do a little meditation on gratitude. Visualize yourself and your beauty, and thank God that your inner light is alchemically charged with love. Let God know you are willing to live a miraculous life. Know that miracles happen whenever love is expressed in its true vibration. Remember that at the heart of any matter is the simple fact that love is the healer.

# The Alchemy of Fate

## *Freeing Our Spirit, Respecting Our Soul*

*Our destiny comes to us from the future.*
*There are, of course, all of the effects of the past—*
*heredity, memory, conditioning, talents, and abilities—*
*and these too work powerfully in our lives.*
*The angels, however, are primarily concerned*
*with our future, individually as well as with*
*the future of humanity and the future of the world.*
*Working with the angels implies learning to care*
*for what is not yet present, but what is coming to be.*
　　　　　　　　　　　　　　　—Robert Sardello

$I$f everything is destined to happen in a certain way, why should we even bother praying? Who controls our destiny? Do we, or is everything set up beforehand and we just go along filling in the picture? On some level, this is a ridiculous question that can only be answered by God, but that doesn't mean we can't speculate or come up with theories. My theory, or current way of responding to this question, has to do with the difference between soul and spirit.

When I first became "serious" about my spiritual path, I went in the direction of spirit, which means I wanted to transcend all things earthly and ego-based. Through meditation, visualization, and prayer, I attempted to rise above myself and connect with the unitive state of Godhead, or the collective consciousness. I really thought that by doing this I would not have any of the problems and struggles that everyday life brought my way. Life would be blissful and free from human struggle.

What actually happened was I found new struggles and problems, and they seemed even more crucial because I thought I was doing all the right spiritual things. Instead of seeming lighter, my life was feeling heavier. I kept praying and meditating. One day, in a very simple way, with no blaring trumpets or fanfare, the angels sent a message to me that changed everything. As I was sitting reading in my quest for enlightenment, I came across a quotation by G. K. Chesterton: "Angels can fly because they take themselves lightly." This little saying hit my consciousness like a blast of light; the room I was sitting in actually looked lighter. I put the book I was reading down and stayed with this new feeling. Two very important things occurred to me. First, I realized I was taking my life way too seriously and not respecting the lighter side, the humorous side, of God. Second, I realized that I was forgetting that the angels are our spiritual helpers in life. When we follow a spiritual path, we are walking with the angels. I had always believed in angels, but now I had an expanded idea of what the angels really do.

Along with my expanded view of angels and divine humor came a deeper appreciation for life on Earth and the importance of soul. To me, soul represents our anchor to this life — our attachment and our "fate." Ironically, the angels, who could be thought of as pure spirit, helped me find my soul and honor the importance of being human. Both spirit and soul are important, and they sometimes seem to be in conflict, but they don't have to be when we learn to honor both. We must each do this in our own way, because each human path is unique.

So, again we face the idea of fate versus free will. The soul has certain things it is programmed to experience. Some explanations for this range from reincarnation, astrology, or the unique experience of our own DNA encoded with messages from our ancestors. The explanations are not the most important thing, just the acknowledgment that your soul holds the key to how you are drawn mysteriously along in life, finding yourself in so many amazing situations, some of which you are sure you wouldn't have volunteered for.

Spirit represents our free will, the idea that we are not locked into any one particular destiny or way of being. Through spirit, we can lift ourselves out of the "wheel of karma." Too much striving to go beyond our soul, beyond our attachment to life, through using our free will to bypass lessons, will create an imbalance. In other words, although we "create" our own destiny by our choices and attitude, there are things we are here to experience. The experiences of the soul are not always charming, and we sometimes wonder why should we have to suffer such trials, but in the long run we will garner from the experience a great truth, and we then will use our spirit to go in a positive direction. Too much spirit brings too much struggle. Too much complacency, however, can make us feel like a "victim" of the soul, of life. As usual we need integration and balance, which we achieve through prayer.

Each life is like a great adventure. Some adventures are obvious, like the life of the movie character Indiana Jones. Others are subtler, calmer. But no matter who we are, we are all on a big adventure. Words used to define *adventure* include "a risky undertaking; a challenging experience; a quest; an unusual and exciting experience; an escapade." The word *escapade* comes from the same origin as the word *escape.* If a fish spends all of its time in the water, would it know that there is anything else? We have all heard the saying "Go with the flow," although recently the saying

"Only dead fish go with the flow" has appeared on T-shirts and posters. When I first heard of this silly little saying, it was so freeing for me. I began exploring the idea that if we always go with the flow, we are like dead fish. Our spirit dies when we just sit back, swallowing everything whole, gulping water, getting knocked around by life, going onward to who knows where. Soon after hearing this humorous saying, I went fly-fishing for the first time, and, besides having a great time, I found myself standing very still in the middle of one of the most beautiful streams in the world, watching how fish actually do go downstream. They *don't* go with the flow. They dart around, they swim across currents, they explore, and occasionally they bite the wrong fly!

Sometimes on our adventure called life we need to get out of—we need to escape—that proverbial flowing river and see what the land is like. Sometimes we may lead others there, too. This is when the journey gets really exciting because we are venturing into uncharted territory. Even a dead fish can't go with the flow on land. So we must be awake and aware, and know that we have inner guides and a guardian angel, and we must talk to the Great Creator through prayer to help us choose the right actions, to help us go in the direction of our heart's true desire. All of this is food for thought; I will leave you here on the land to play with the concept in your own adventurous way.

I sometimes think that I am kidding myself when I tell myself that I have made certain choices based on situations and then look back on my life and it appears that something else was making choices for me. I propose that perhaps we operate on different levels of our psyche, which are not in the forefront of our waking consciousness. So one part of our psyche may guide us into situations for our growth, or away from situations that we claim to want but that would not be truly right for us. I firmly believe that there are certain patterns in ourselves that we are here on Earth to change, and these patterns also reflect the collective psyche. I also believe that there are ancestral patterns that we have been born into that we can change to create a better future. We cannot be dead fish in these matters, for patterns are difficult to change; they are strong currents that we must swim against. The most challenging aspect to our great adventure is doing what we came here to do. The great gift is that we can have moments of true enjoyment, of ecstasy, and of deep love even in the midst of solving problems and learning lessons, but only if we are truly awake and doing our inner work.

I began this chapter with the question "If everything is destined to happen in a certain way, why should we even bother praying?" The answer to every spiritual question, in my opinion, has something to do with love. Love is always our saving grace, and it is our true reason for existing. To love "correctly," we need extra help from the Great Creator of Love. We get this by praying for the highest way of action, of love. We are often inclined to pray to stop "bad things from happening to good people." This is a noble cause, but it doesn't always work, and it may not always be right, or truly for "the highest good," because our idea of what is bad for others might actually provide the trigger for their spiritual transformation, something their souls need to experience in order to grow. So, what do we do in a situation where we feel that we need to change destiny? First, I suggest we pray for God's will to be done. And then, second, we can use the words "If it be the correct action, I pray that . . ." This issue touches on another one of those fine lines having to do with how to help others — or ourselves.

Human destiny is a confusing subject because there are so many variables that move us along our path. These variables include other people, major decisions, the weather, forces of history, and so on. It may not be in our power to understand completely what may be destined to happen, or why, but to assist in anything different happening is a matter for the alchemy of prayer. Destiny changes when we turn our lead to gold. The more gold we introduce into our consciousness, the more conscious we are of our work for God. Our work for God arises out of deep love.

Every time a human takes the risk to experience deep love, a new imprint goes forth into the universe that others may use to guide their own experience of deep love, at which time they expand the imprint, and more love is created for everyone. This is a difficult concept to explain and follow, but I know it is true. Each of us has the chance to make a positive and important effect on the world's soul when we choose to share our love in the most creative way possible. This is why prayer is so effective; it sends out a thought form into the universe that blazes a trail for the highest good to happen. I also believe that when two people make a commitment to love each other and go deeply into the heart of love, they are blazing a trail that others can follow. As Paramahansa Yogananda's master once said, "The deeper the Self-realization of a man, the more he influences the whole universe by his subtle spiritual vibrations, and the less he himself is affected by the phenomenal flux."

### Understanding Our Place in Cosmic Evolution

• Each moment is a collective decision involving us and God. The future of the planet and all of the many aspects of life on Earth require us to do our best and to pray. When we pray, regardless of the contents of the prayers themselves, we are helping evolution. Being true to who we are is better than being "right" yet insincere. We are here to evolve. So be true to yourself, strive to know God's will, and then offer your heartfelt prayers to God. Remember to listen for the answers.

• When you are at an impasse in your life, whether it be in a relationship or regarding a spiritual question, pray to God and ask that you be shown the best way to love.

# The Alchemy of Humility

## *Honoring Our Inner Light*

*Human survival depends on whether we are*
*brave enough to face the full desolation of*
*what we have done to our psyches and the planet,*
*and wise and humble enough to turn*
*to the Divine inside and outside us*
*to learn what we will need to go forward.*

—**Andrew Harvey**

*B*eing human is a complex experience to say the least. Awakening our spiritual nature gives us a view of being human that goes beyond our physical space and our selfish desires. If we don't redefine ourselves once we begin awakening, huge conflicts arise in our lives. One of the biggest has to do with pride. Pride is a mixed bag, in that we need to feel proud once in a while, but being proud can mean being stubbornly attached to a narrow point of view. We can change the chemistry of the "feeling" of pride to consciously loving the divine within us. Instead of feeling proud that we did something great, we acknowledge the Divine Creator and give thanks that we are gifted with the ability to transform the world with love through the guidance of the heavens. In other words, we constantly acknowledge that our time here on Earth is by the grace of God. It is sacred time, and we stand on holy ground, with our body as a temple in which the Light of God dwells.

Etymologically, the word *humble* means close to the ground and comes from *humus,* the Latin word for Earth. There is no way to ignore how humble—how close to the ground—we truly are. Human life is an Earth experience. The humus, the soil of the Earth, is what sustains us. Our bodies are made from the same elements of the ground on which we build houses, pave roads, destroy forests, and fashion comfort for our survival. We can spend most of our time here trying to escape in one way or another, but the fact is that the human race has very little chance of survival if there is not a massive spiritual transformation of values—a letting go of the excessive pride of thinking that humans are all-powerful. Mother Nature humbles us often. Earthquakes, storms, and a basic understanding of her natural laws make us realize how powerless we are in the face of our changing planet. Sometimes we may experience fear as we contemplate these powerful forces.

Fear can be crippling or it can be positively motivating. When we are not dealing consciously with fear, it moves us into prideful ways of being. For example, our fear of being hurt by people may cause us to become racists if we do not change the chemistry of that fear. Whatever we fear may in some ways be a real threat, yet when we turn our lives over to God, then the fear of the threat is worse than the threat itself. This does not mean that we will be completely untouched by harmful intentions. One of the things that makes the angels weep, one of the things that fills the land with sadness, is when humans use their free will to intentionally hurt others and themselves. Part of being humble is acknowledging our fears and realizing the truth that life is full of danger. The wonderful part is that, with the strength of God within us, this danger can provide the very fuel that leads us to greatness, especially when we pray for this. Prayer can transform fear into humility and courage.

The vital signs of the planet are in a critical state, and all that we do and think affects the direction of our dear planet. If you think that negative thought forms don't have a disastrous effect on the planet, simply because thoughts are not tangible, then you are kidding yourself and are full of false pride. Our thoughts and desires are shaping the planet every day. Hatred is an energy that goes out into the psyche of the world and has the effect of making the angels cry. If that image is not powerful enough to convince you that hate has an impact, I don't know what could be. I am not writing about this to make anyone feel bad about themselves or bad about being a human. Rather, I am leading up to one of the most important things I think we as individuals can do to "save the humans," and that is attain enough humility to go within ourselves and do some powerful alchemy in the form of inner work, the topic of the next chapter. If we are on the side of God and the angels, God will be on our side, and the angels will be our companions. If we choose to go against the grain, to disobey spiritual laws, then Lucifer, the fallen archangel, will be our guide. The choice is now presented to us—the dark and the light are greatly polarized—but we have to be awake and conscious as we choose our direction.

I think our first real glimpse of being awake, of being conscious, comes through humility. Humility, like gratitude, is a powerful alchemical essence. When we truly humble ourselves, and get down on our knees on the sacred humus, then we are raised up in spirit to unimaginable heights. We must sometimes go down before we can go up. We must often go within before we can operate consciously outside. Humility is an ongoing process for us to open to, and the best way is through prayer, through communication with God. Prayer with humility and gratitude offers a direct, alchemical pathway to spiritual gold. Prepare your inner soil and give the humus of your soul the humble richness it needs to present you with the real treasures of heaven.

### Humbling Yourself Without Humiliation

• Pray to know the difference between humiliation and humility, and walk that fine line, especially in your dealings with others.

• We sometimes pray on our knees as an act of humility. Visualize yourself praying in a kneeling position, or actually get down on your knees. If you have a personal altar or shrine in your house, kneel in front of it. Pray to God in the form of the Divine Feminine, whatever that may mean to you. Think of humility and what it means to you, and ask that Feminine Wisdom to grant you the grace of humility. The feminine side of God, says, "Thou mayest" instead of "Thou shalt." Contemplate the essence of "Thou mayest." Let it permeate your soul, and then give thanks. This will create alchemy in your humble soul.

• Humble yourself with the knowledge that you are a part of God, and notice how you treat God in yourself. Sincere humility includes recognizing the truth that all life is one, all life is part of God, and that includes you. Do you treat yourself as you would God? Honor your inner light; it is there because you are a child of God. Remember also that our humility is for God, not for humanity. We must be humble in the light, not the shadows.

Leonard Cohen explores this idea and leaves us with some great images in his writing "In the Eyes of Men": "But he falls radiantly toward the light to which he falls. They cannot see who lifts him as he falls, or how his falling changes, and he himself bewildered till his heart cries out to bless the one who holds him in his fallings. And in his fall he hears his heart cry out, his heart explains why he is falling, why he had to fall, and he gives over to the fall. Blessed are you, clasp of the falling. He falls into the sky, he falls into the light, no one can hurt his fall, concealed within his fall, he finds the place, he is gathered in. While his hair streams back and his clothes tear in the wind, he is held up, comforted, he enters into the place of his fall. Blessed are you, embrace of the falling, foundation of light, master of the human accident."

# PART THREE

# HOLY SPIRIT WITHIN

### *The Fire of God*

*At the core of our being*
*Burns a divine flame.*
*The Holy Spirit lives in each of us.*
*Knowing ourselves, doing our inner work,*
*Leads us to the serenity of mental peace.*
*Once we attain mental peace,*
*We also find courage and personal power.*
*Love glows as a warm flame in our heart,*
*forever fueled by the breath of God.*

# The Alchemy of Inner Work

## *"Know Thyself"*

*Through the mystery of this inner work*
*darkness is turned into light.*
*The chaos and confusion of our unconscious*
*. . . gradually and miraculously reveal*
*a higher centre of consciousness which is*
*none other than our innermost essence,*
*"the face we had before we were born."*
*This is the Self, the Divine Child,*
*which was always present within us,*
*but hidden beneath layers of ego and conditioning.*
—Llewellyn Vaughan-Lee

*P*rayer is a form of therapy and inner work. When we pray, we begin to change our chemistry on an inner level whether we are aware of it or not. Three main things are asked of us spiritually these days: that we stay awake, that we know ourselves, and that we develop an unbounded trust in God. The Buddha was once asked, "Are you an angel?" The Buddha answered, "No." He was next asked, "Are you then a god?" Again the Buddha answered, "No." "What are you then?" he was asked. "I am simply awake," he replied. If you are familiar with the Buddha's story, you know he had to do a great deal of inner work, facing his inner "demons" and illusions head-on to achieve this awake state. Such a state does not come easily.

I sometimes avoid using the word *work,* or when I do use it I put a slash next to it and write *work/play.* I am not against work, but sometimes the idea of it gives us a sense of defeat before we ever begin. Work denotes how and where we direct our energy. Play is also a matter of directing energy, and our "work" can take on a new chemistry when we allow our work energy to be playful and exploratory. Perhaps the scariest territory to explore is our individuality and the inside of our minds and souls. It may be ironic, but we may need the most courage ever in our lives to face ourselves and know ourselves. And we have a choice to be playful with all of this.

When we pray for transformation, we don't necessarily change outwardly. Rather, it is more that we come into our own; we metamorphose into that proverbial butterfly. The seeds of the butterfly were in us all along. There comes a point in each life when we create the right conditions to let those seeds germinate and grow into the magnificent creature that we are. Sometimes our soul lets us know it is time for transformation. The chances for living a deeper, more aware, and more meaningful life come our way in each moment. When we are aware of ourselves and our patterns, then we will recognize and listen to the messages our soul is bringing to us.

Awareness means being mindful, conscious, cognizant— possessing a knowingness of what is happening on the inner and outer levels of our being. Knowing something means we are aware of it, and we allow it to have many levels of discovery. Awareness is the most powerful tool humans possess as far as spiritual, personal, and physical growth go. Healing happens through awareness. The reason awareness is so powerful is that once we are aware of something we can never go back and do it in the same way. We need courageous awareness and an intention of staying fully awake through pain and joy to do our inner work. We get courage when we create a deep prayer connection with God, so that we can ask for transformation and be willing to evolve. Now we return to the issue of pain. As we know, growth can be painful, but labor pains bring the joy of birth.

When I was about five years old, one of my most earnest prayers was asking God to remove all pain, for all people, from all the things that could hurt us. I was especially concerned with physical pain and was hoping my prayers would lead to a time that when I skinned my knee while riding my bike, it wouldn't hurt. My father was listening to my prayers one night and heard me asking this. He gently made me understand how important it is that we feel pain when we get hurt so that we can tend to the wound and keep it from getting worse while we help it heal. He also said that it was important to feel pain in certain situations so that we wouldn't repeat them. I can't say that I fully understood the whole gist of our conversation on pain when I was five, but it stayed with me, and eventually I came to understand very clearly the importance of pain.

Last year I had an accident in which a window fell on my left hand, crushing two of my fingers. This happened on a Saturday morning, so I knew that my doctor wouldn't be in. I was adamantly repelled by the idea of an emergency room visit. This "little" accident happened at a most crucial time. I had papers due for a class I was taking and a major book to write, along with a typically long list of "things to do," and I went into shock at the overwhelming physical pain of my hurt fingers and the emotional stress of the implications of what this was going to mean in my everyday life. The first thing I did was take a shower; I just wanted to be in water. Then I called a friend and told her what had happened. She suggested that I take some Bach Flower Rescue Remedy (which I really believe in) orally and also that I put some on my fingers. After I did this, I decided to take a nap.

Taking a nap posed an interesting problem. I was in so much pain that sleeping seemed impossible, and I had to keep my hand in a certain position or it felt like it would throb right off my arm. What I did next was to quiet my mind, say a prayer, and take myself right into the very source of the pain. This wasn't easy, but I kept at it until I knew I was in complete alignment with the pain coming from the damaged nerves in my fingers. When I reached this point, I fell asleep. Of course, I am not suggesting that everyone follow my course of action; there are certainly times to visit emergency rooms, and even in this case, several of my friends thought I was crazy not to have gone. When Monday morning came and I finally went to visit my doctor, he sent me downstairs from his office to get x-rays. The x-ray doctor told my doctor that he had no idea how I had gotten through the weekend without major pain medicine, because the fracture to my two fingers was so severe that most people would have collapsed from the pain.

I am using my story as a metaphor of what we are capable of doing with pain. Alchemy happens when we go to the wound for our healing. My pain subsided enough for me to sleep when I took my point of consciousness to the site of my most intense pain. When we choose to heal—when we choose to become whole—we have to bring into view all that is us, and our wounds are a living part of us, too. Instead of trying to cut them out and ignore them, consider asking that they bring you insight and teaching. If you are in pain physically or struggling with something emotionally, allow it to evolve by being there with it. Feelings are not barometers of actual moments of truth; feelings pass and change. Pray not that the pain cease but that you somehow honor its message the same way you would a message from an angel. Pain doesn't last; it is like a forming bud on a fruit tree, and its fragrant blossom is joy. We won't get the fruit if we cut off the bud of pain.

When we pray in the spirit of inner work, we are praying to know all the parts of ourselves. The saying goes: "Know yourself and you will know how to live." Emerson once said: "Trust thyself: every heart vibrates to that inner string." There are many ways to the self, and many parts of ourselves waiting to be acknowledged. We are here to be ourselves, and our beauty comes to the surface when we align ourselves with our *own* divine spark of life, a spark that shines in its own special way.

In his book *Love and the Soul*, Robert Sardello writes: "Beauty is not an accidental quality of the rose, but the rose being a rose, doing what a rose does. Individuality acts in a similar manner; that is, individuality is not something one has or even something one is, an individual. Individuality is an act—the act of inner, conscious awareness shaping, forming and interiorizing the essence of each moment of experience, endowing experience with reverence and love, thereby individualizing what presents itself to consciousness." We have to understand that when we pray, regardless of what we are asking for, somewhere in our psyche a voice is calling out for the transformation that leads to individuality, to knowing ourselves.

We have inner tools available to us at all times, but tools can't build anything when they sit unused. Journal keeping is a great way to get to know ourselves. Telling our story, our true story, is important, because telling it can heal others when we have ventured to the heart of who we are. There is instant alchemy in *facing* fear, as opposed to being paralyzed by or avoiding fear. We can start by sharing our fears with God through prayer. We can ask for extra courage in a situation, for the strength and faith to rise above whatever seems threatening to us. This is so simple, but many people can't seem to do it. In the beginning, inner work and facing the unknown parts of us are a little like learning to swim when you are afraid of the water. So approach the situation gingerly. Get to know the properties of the water before you try and swim in it. Don't go into the basement unless you have built a strong foundation for your house. Our lives need a foundation, and we achieve this when we pray and get to know God in our own special way.

Another great tool for inner work is dream awareness. Pray for healing dreams each night before you go to sleep. We are given access to the deepest parts of our consciousness each night, and the chance to allow our imagination total freedom, for there is no way for our waking mind to try its control tactics while we sleep. If you can get into the habit of remembering your dreams and writing them down, you will be amazed by the changes in your waking consciousness.

A ritual is another powerful healing tool when performed with the intention of restoring balance. It can be very simple, or it can involve detailed ceremony. Humans are naturally ritualistic; we perform little rituals all the time without being aware of them. We sometimes ignore ritual when we need it the most. When I get in a quandary and want to change the chemistry of a situation, I perform a ritual. I create a sense of sacred space by praying for it, and then I simply start to dialogue with the part of myself that seems to be hiding the very things that are creating the "problem." Usually I write while I do this process; other times I may do it in my mind.

Here is an example of such a dialogue: "I am at a gate. I ask, 'Who is my guide today? Who out there has a message for me?' I receive no answer, so I state my intentions.

'I come seeking a sorting of my feelings, then a view of my appointment with destiny.' Hawk appears. I ask, 'What truth am I not seeing clearly, Hawk?'" Once I have an image of the nature of my guide, many interesting insights begin to emerge; my energy shifts dramatically.

If we know a tried-and-true way of getting somewhere, we may never venture off the beaten path, where a revelation or experience that could change our life might be waiting. We naturally look for safety in life — a safe way to be brave. Not many of us volunteer to venture into those dark places of our soul where the vision of our magic lives, because we know there is a chance we will get scorched by the fire that burns within us. We need to be taught how to use our inner resources, and this happens through the lessons we incur. The flame burning in our soul is there to keep us awake, alive, and warm. Fire needs air to burn. If we keep our inner fire too far out of reach, it will not have enough air to burn, and our spirit will start to atrophy. The choice is ours: We can wake up and acquire "the eyes to see and the ears to hear," or we can put parts of ourselves to sleep and miss out on the true ecstasy of God.

The main point of this chapter is to encourage you to integrate your inner life with your perceived outer life. Inner work brings us insight. When we know ourselves at the deepest level, we know God. Learn who is within you.

The answers to your prayers can be found when you venture inward and acknowledge all the aspects that make you who you are. True alchemical change takes place as you look inside yourself using the magic ingredient—love. When we love something, we rise to the occasion.

### Journeying to Your Center

• Pray for the strength to go within and connect with your inner dimensions. Learn to understand your own energy field, and pay attention to patterns you may want to change. Remember that the goal of inner work is to know God and therefore to know and trust yourself better, and achieve a state of inner mental peace.

• Keep a journal to record your inner work; it can serve as a touchstone for the rest of your life.

• Pay attention to your dreams. One form of dream interpretation invites you to consider all the characters in your dream as parts of yourself and then attempt to "own" them.

• One way to start an active-imagination dialogue is to ask your pain what it wants from you or ask a guide to appear to answer your questions. If you are dialoging with a part of yourself you are unfamiliar with, it may take a great deal of energy to let it speak. It takes courage to meet unknown parts of yourself, but the process brings you face-to-face with your own special magic.

• Rainer Maria Rilke, in *Letters to a Young Poet*, once wrote: "A work of art is good if it has sprung from necessity. In this nature of its origin lies the judgment of it: there is no other. Therefore, my dear sir, I know no advice for you save this: to go into yourself and test the deeps in which your life takes rise; at its source you will find the answer to the question whether you *must* create. Accept it, just as it sounds, without inquiring into it. Perhaps it will turn out that you are called to be an artist. Then take that destiny upon yourself and bear it, its burden and its greatness, without ever asking what recompense might come from outside. For the creator must be a world for himself and find everything in himself." Reflect on this quotation as you explore ways your inner work can add dimension to your prayer life.

# The Alchemy of Mental Peace

## *Generating Serenity*

*Whatever the art you may wish to learn*
*—whether it be acrobatics or violin playing,*
*mental prayer or golf, acting, singing,*
*dancing or what you will—*
*there is one thing that every*
*good teacher will always say:*
*Learn to combine relaxation with activity;*
*learn to do what you have to do*
*without strain;*
*work hard, but never under tension.*
—Aldous Huxley

*D*o you ever get that feeling of being uncomfortable, of not being at home in your body? When this happens, most of us feel angst and agitation coursing through our bloodstream. Everything seems to bother us; our soul seems restless and our spirit spooked like a wild mustang in a wind storm. As a family friend Vern Faulstich used to say, "It's time to bring your ship into calm waters." Angst entails anxiety and anguish, and it can seem to have a life of its own. When it comes to visit, it looks for a place in your body to reside. It may settle in your shoulders and give you a tight feeling. It may toss around in your stomach and give you heartburn. It seeks to disturb your mind. It has a message when it comes to visit. The message will be personal to you, but always indicates a time to pray for inner peace, sort out some issues, and burn off the dross.

When angst takes over, we often want to run out and spend time with people or engage in some activity to make it go away. This only fuels the angst. The best way to give angst less room in your consciousness is to be alone with it and bring peace to fill the spaces it wants to occupy. By doing the thing that seems most difficult, we change the chemistry. When we are feeling agitated, it is as if our inner flame is being blown around by too much wind. Picture what this would look like. Some things might catch on fire that you don't want to have burn, and then the wind could blow the flame away from the very things that need warmth.

When this happens, our first and wisest step can be to go into prayer and visualize the holy peace of God calming our soul and spirit, bringing comfort to our body, and tempering our inner flame. Next, we can pay attention to messages we may receive that inspire us in the direction of faith and peace.

Anxiety can be the result of unexpressed fears. When you pray, express your fears regardless of how small or large they are. Worry and anxiety concern the future, but they use up energy in the present. Jesus said, "And which of you by worrying and being anxious can add one measure to his stature or to the span of his life?" (Matthew 6:28). When we are in the grips of worrying, we need to think of this question about what exactly the worrying is doing for us. It is important not to berate ourselves for worrying, for there are many things that naturally cause us to worry. The wisest course of action is to turn the worry into creative thinking, and then let it go in your prayers after you are done thinking about it.

My friend Jai told me a story while I was writing this chapter, not knowing that I was writing about worry. She was responding to my telling her that I cannot help but worry when someone I love is traveling. She agreed that it is difficult not to worry but added, "You either have worry or you have faith; you can't have both." Then she told me about the first time she really had to choose between worry and faith. Her son was six years old, and they lived at the top of a mountain. One day, her son wanted to ride his bike down the hill to visit a friend. Jai knew she had to say yes, but after he took off down the road and she went inside to wash dishes, fear struck her heart. She just knew something bad was going to happen to him. Then she had the feeling that God was sending her a message with the thought: "Do not project fear into the situation; let it go and put your trust in God." Well, her son made it down the mountain, although he did fall and hurt his knee. He got right back up on his bike and continued on to his friend's house. When he came back home, he showed Jai his muscles, and she saw the first glimpse of his manhood taking shape. It was an important day for them both.

It is not so difficult to make peace with our worries when we truly understand the ways of God. The process of worrying is actually worse for us than a real traumatic event, because during an event we use our resources for dealing with the event in the moment. The less worry preceding a worrisome event, the more energy we have clear to bring the highest attention possible to the situation. Often our mental peace is thwarted because we worry about things that are beyond our control, such as other people's destiny, the weather, or circumstances that just are what they are. At these times, it is important to pray for release from your worries, to "let go and let God." And always remember that you have an endless source of creativity available to tap into when you need to jump into action in response to any situation.

To achieve a state of mental peace, we can pray for and be open to knowing contentment. Contentment is a state of mind that goes with inner peace. When we are content, we have a profound level of comfort in our mind, body, spirit, and soul. A deep sense of satisfaction comes to us that is not dependent on outside circumstances, such as making more money or having more material possessions. This satisfaction comes from deep inside us because we know the ways of God. Once we touch this level of comfort, we will know it is always there for us. When we understand that we can calm our minds and connect with God, anyplace, anytime, we can achieve contentment regardless of the drama going on around us.

A Chinese proverb says: "Only the contented are magnanimous." To be magnanimous means that one is generous, high-minded, noble, and forgiving, never petty. The Latin root for *magnanimous* means large-minded. The word *magnificent* comes from the same root, and means doing great deeds. In the Bible, Mary says: "My soul magnifies and extols the Lord." Cultivating magnanimity is like sprinkling gold dust on our inner spiritual flame. When we allow our center to be nourished with high, exalted thinking and noble behavior, we magnify the Lord, and in the most natural way we will do great deeds. Our warmth will precede us, and the angels will go before us, sprinkling the way with divine sparks of inspiration for the world to witness.

Once we truly practice letting God take care of our greatest concerns, we achieve serenity. Serenity combines the qualities of acceptance, gratitude, tranquillity, and deep peace. One moment of true serenity gives us more wisdom and grace than anything else. Serenity gives us the foundation we need to truly love from our heart center. Exploring the beauty of silence brings us closer to serenity in our lives. Silence is more than a lack of noise. Silence is God's peace, God's heartbeat. We can only know silence when we quiet our minds: "Be still and know that God is within you."

### Serenity as Your Ever-Present Pilot Flame

• Find a place you love in nature and go there often. While you are there, listen to the silence of nature. Let nature enter your soul and speak to you. Fall in love with a tree.

• Calm down and take a love bath. Pray for inner peace once an hour, and you will see changes taking place in your soul. Learn to be alone and love it; love you. Cherish moments spent in solitude. Know that silence is pure magic.

• Learn to carry peace around with you. Know that when you are with those who have restless souls, a little glimpse of your serenity will calm them down. Ask the angels to help permeate the consciousness of those you meet who need peace in their hearts.

• Think about the idea of being good-natured. Being good-natured means having an easygoing, cheerful, tolerant disposition. Being good-natured is permanently with you; it is habitual and comes from a calm and centered mind. It is natural. We can also be good-humored, which also means being cheerful, but has to do with our spirit (and humors) more than with our innate disposition. The point is that inner peace runs deep into our nature and the gifts are good.

• Let your soul magnify, glorify, celebrate, and extol the Lord!

# The Alchemy of Personal Power

## *Transforming Sensitivity*

*You are the salt of the earth,*
*but if salt has lost its taste*
*— its strength, its quality —*
*how can its saltiness be restored?*
*It is not good for anything*
*any longer but to be thrown out*
*and trodden under foot by men.*
*You are the light of the world.*
*A city set on a hill cannot be hid.*
*Nor do men light a lamp and put it under*
*a peck-measure but on a lamp stand,*
*and it gives light to all in the house.*
Matthew 5:13–15

Our sensitivity can be our greatness if we have the strength of God within us, or it can slowly drain us until we are of no use, just like the salt spoken of above.

Prayer can give us the strength to let our light shine and the wherewithal to overcome our fears of what other people may try to do to our light.

Each of us carries around a signature presence. Presence is a matter of the present moment; having presence means we are here now, awake and alive, being us. Presence is an authentic response to life. There is no way to lie to God in our prayers and in our actions. When we are authentic, we are our own authority and become the original author of our own life. This is where our personal power comes from. To feel powerful in life, as opposed to victimized at each turn, we need to confront our sensitivity and personal responses, and strengthen our presence with God's love.

Have you ever thought that you are just too sensitive for life on Earth? Have you thought that being sensitive is a curse? Well, sensitivity is actually a sacred gift. But, it is difficult to cherish and protect one's innate gift of sensitivity in a noisy and sometimes offensive world. We can change the chemistry of our sensitivity into strength and personal power when we integrate the tool of prayer. People who are sensitive often take on more than they can handle because they sense the feelings of others and want to respond to them. Such people pick up the nuances of situations. It is as if the pain of others is screaming at them, demanding attention.

So, what can we do when we feel helpless in a situation with another member of our species? We can pray with our guardian angel. Our guardian angel is very willing to connect with another person's guardian angel and help the situation take a turn for the highest good of all. Just as we like to help others when a disaster strikes, our angels like to help one another, too. So, if we send out prayers through our guardian angel, waves of love bless and change the situation. We need true discernment about when to help another or when to get involved in another person's life issues. As sensitive people, we have deep compassion and want to alleviate the suffering of others. This is truly a noble gesture, but it can end up causing more suffering if we are not careful. Rescue a victim, and you can become a victim of the victim. Help people too much with their careers, and you rob them of the chance to make things happen on their own. When we try to make things happen for others, we rob the angels of the chance to help them be just where they need to be.

In certain aboriginal cultures, one of the worst offenses or crimes you can commit is dream stealing, which can be punishable by banishment from your tribe. An example of dream stealing would be if I were to tell you about what I want to create in the future, and you were to say, "Oh, there's no way you could possibly do that," or "That is the craziest idea I have ever heard!" Well, I am sure you can relate to how prevalent dream stealing is in our culture, and there are certainly no laws against it. There is another crime we commit regularly in our society, and that is pain stealing. Pain is what teaches us and what gives us character, and each time we try to ease other people's pain, we rob them of a chance to discover a message from their soul. This is a tricky concept, and it takes a good deal of thought and consciousness to put into practice. Emotional pain and suffering are so hard to deal with in ourselves and to witness in others. But regardless of the situation, there are some times when people need to honor their own pain, and we are wise to allow them the freedom to do so. Even and especially if others are trying to blame you for their pain, this is a signal to leave them on their own.

Get to a point where the tragedies and personal issues of others do not strike a personal note and bring on your own personal drama. Let people honor their own pain without removing it for them or suffering over something that does not belong to you. Don't steal others' suffering. We don't need to project ourselves into another's tragedy; that takes away the real strength we need for helping the highest good come to pass through our prayers. To act with compassion, think of what God would do. Do not try to fix things immediately when you may not understand exactly what is broken.

It is important that we understand the obvious about energy. There are many ways to enter into energy imbalances with others. It helps to understand and recognize them so we can avoid them. When we seek to get an energy boost from another person, some of that person's energy is going to come to us. Sometimes people offer up their energy to us, by asking us for advice or help with a situation, and often this ends up draining us. The key is to know that all energy comes from God; to recharge our own inner battery means going to God first and foremost for our energy.

Some people are agitators, and others are peacemakers. Sometimes it is difficult to recognize agitators because they are disguised as interesting or highly conscious people and seem to be interested in the peace of all. Sometimes agitators may not even know that they have an agitating effect on others; they may only know that they like to stir things up. Drama is somehow created around them. Agitators will drain us if we let them. It is our responsibility to recognize the feeling we get around others, then make the choice of how to handle it and personally respond while keeping in mind that we cannot control their behavior. To agitate means to disturb and cause anxiety. To know if others are causing agitation in your life, think about how you feel after a simple discussion with them. How do they leave you feeling? Think about how *you* leave others feeling. In peace or upset?

Most of all, it is important for sensitive people to do the thing hardest for them—to think of themselves first, which in reality is thinking of God first. You have gifts that you are here to develop. No one gains when these gifts are wasted on futile attempts to save others, or when you feel bombarded by life. If we keep our inner flame healthy and strong, we will be able to ride the waves of tension and uncertainty to the shore of love. If we are out of balance, we will fall into the turbulent surf and flounder around. Keep yourself strong and powerful. You are shouldered with a great responsibility by being sensitive: You are part of a force fighting to keep beauty and love from becoming extinct on our planet. The angels are here to help, and God loves you; your sensitivity is truly a gift when you pray for discernment. Use prayer as your path to compassion. Whenever you feel the need to help another, pray in earnest first that the highest and most correct course of action be taken.

## Soothing Your Sensitive Soul

### *Beauty*

• I can only be inspired to write when I know I am immersed in beauty. Beauty is a healing force. Beauty is the energy of angels dancing in our spirit. Pray to know and exercise beauty in your own special way.

### *Music*

• Don't forget the cosmic dance, the language of the heart, the choirs of the angels. When you need an instant chemistry change, put on some beautiful music and let your soul dance and connect with that awesome love. Send it out to others. Beautiful music is immaculate prayer.

### *Rest*

• Get enough rest. Sleep isn't always restful. Think about true rest. Take restful naps when you need to. Go into your private space, and learn to take restful time-outs from the noise of life. Surround yourself in the peace of God by praying for deep rest. Allow God's love to hold you and melt away all your worries.

# PART FOUR

# INSPIRED REVERENCE

### *Inspiration Is God's Breath*

*With the angels' guidance,*
*We are inspired to find our strong center.*
*We practice the true compassion*
*Of loving behavior and generosity.*
*We share our prayer alchemy*
*And create more love in the world*
*From a place of deep reverence.*
*We become prayer in action.*
*Love is in the air;*
*Take a deep breath.*
*Be still and know in your heart*
*That God is ever present within you.*

# The Alchemy of Loving Behavior

## Compassion

*The things that matter most in our lives*
*are not fantastic or grand.*
*They are the moments*
*when we touch one another,*
*when we are there*
*in the most attentive or caring way.*
—Jack Kornfield

If I had to choose one concept in this book that I most wanted people to understand, it would be the simple truth that God responds to the love we generate and keep in our hearts. Without love, whatever we do for God doesn't shine. Perhaps we all know this, but do we live it? One way to keep this perspective is to imagine that at the end of your life, God will ask this question: *How well did you love?* You may face other questions as well: Did you risk anything to love? Did you live fully, dance and sing when inspired, give the world your best? I doubt we will be asked how much money we made or how many greedy deals we won.

Love is both a behavior and a choice. It is something that we need to show to others, and to *act* upon when we are deeply moved by its power. Often we get into relationships before we are truly willing to love. We don't seem to understand what love actually entails. We may think that we are ready to be loved, that love will do everything for us and we can simply sit back and catch the rays. In his book *Love and the Soul*, Robert Sardello discusses how we often expect to be *carried* by love, when we really need to be *creating* love. He writes, "We are entering a time, an epoch, in which love must be created, and created in relation not only one to another but in relation to the world."

Examine for a moment how you like to be shown love. Do you like to be flattered and worshipped, or do you respond to simple acts of caring that you know come from the heart of another? Often we let our mind rule the way we accept love, instead of our heart. Our mind wants proof of love; our heart simply responds to the love. If we are to create love, we had better start learning how to love. We need to open our hearts. If the door to your heart is stuck, pry it open; your heart is ready to expand and love, and it cries silently when you ignore it and keep the door closed.

When we are captured by beautiful moments between us and our loved ones, it is tempting to want to possess the beauty, to try and own it in some way. When we approach love as something to own and possess, we enter into a power game. Carl Jung once said: "Where love reigns, there is no will to power; and where the will to power is paramount, love is lacking. The one is but the shadow of the other." When we understand the beauty and light that come to visit us are from God, we will know that there is no need to possess them; they come freely to us whenever we are truly willing to love in the moment, and keep some space open in our hearts for God to join us.

Why does it seem to be so difficult at times to show love and to enjoy this precious gift of life we have been given? We each have many reasons, but there are no real excuses because we can truly "build a bridge and get over" our personal problems if we want to. Even if we have been dealt the worst set of cards possible, there is a gift somewhere in the hand. There are too many examples of people who have had all the odds against them and yet leave trails of love and inspiration behind them wherever they go; thus, I find it hard to believe that there are people who simply cannot behave out of a real space of love.

There are people all around us who have risen to the occasion, gotten away from themselves, and found a way to be truly loving and gracious even in the midst of the most disastrous circumstances. I am not talking about being kind to strangers either; that is too easy. I mean being kind and loving in the most honest way to those closest to us, those upon whom we have the most influence. Let's remember that kindness is honest; it is not just the act of fulfilling people's needs, but being there for them in love. Prayer helps us find this chemistry.

To think that we can love without compassion is like thinking we can purchase love in a store. Compassion is the wish for others to be happy and not suffer, yet the root of the word means "to suffer with." The degree to which we can truly show compassion to others depends upon how well we have embraced our own suffering. To understand compassion, we need to experience our own suffering and loneliness deeply, and then know that others have these same feelings. There are times when we may be sad or feel depressed, and we cannot find an external reason. At such times, we need to honor the sadness, whether or not it has a reason. Feeling bad about feeling bad is not exactly productive. Even when we are sad, we can serve as a loving presence to others if we are honest.

Recognizing our soul's connection to compassion leads us to the awareness that we need to have a deep respect for ourselves before we can reach out and show compassion and kindness to others. The Dalai Lama has said: "Each of us has responsibility for all humankind. It is time for us to think of other people as true brothers and sisters and to be concerned with their welfare, with lessening their suffering. This is my simple religion. There is no need for temples; no need for complicated philosophy. Our own brain, our own heart is our temple; the philosophy is kindness."

The opposite of compassion is hatred. How could we ever think that hating others and punishing them for what they have done could ever really remedy a situation? To treat hate with more hate, and to hurt people who hurt us, perpetuates pain. This happens throughout our society: Kindness is rare; harshness rules. It is important to realize that criticism, a milder cousin to hatred, is deadly to the human spirit. Any society that has designated some people as critics is in trouble. We have to work against the urge to criticize. I catch myself being critical of things and people when it really isn't necessary. So pay attention to your own critical thoughts, and when you are criticized by others, ask in prayer that the words be transmuted and lifted from your spirit.

Prayer offers us a path into a deep response of compassion. Our ability to be compassionate connects us with the soul of the world in a profound way, and combining compassion with prayer can change the world in an instant. When the alchemy of compassion takes hold of our heart, even the most horrendous crime against us can be forgiven. Forgiveness does not mean you have to forget; your energy is best spent on being willing to forgive and finding compassion in your heart, as opposed to forgetting the wrong. It is not always wise to forget harms. We can find a way to love the worst of our enemies, and by doing so we will release a blast of love so pure into the heart of the world that all around us lead will begin to shine like gold. But this alchemy won't happen without prayer. We need God's help to love our fellow human beings, and to think we can do it alone reflects false pride.

Compassion gives us reverence, a profound respect for life. When we are reverent, it is not possible for us to exploit others; we honor life and connect with the essence of the life force. Reverent people know there is something deep inside of each living creature that carries the spirit of God, something that is sacred. Reverence entails deep acceptance — not a judgment of whether something is holy. It means we are honoring the "Buddha nature" of all things, knowing that each has its sacred purpose.

With compassion, not only do we want to alleviate the suffering of others, we also want them to have happiness. This sacred dimension of compassion means we need happiness also. Often it seems as if true happiness is the most difficult thing to attain. When you feel far away from happiness, it is time to pray and tell God that you want to *know* happiness, to understand the nature of being happy. If you continue to pray with thanksgiving and faith for the essence of happiness to come into your life, it will. Happiness has its own timing; it may seem elusive, but it is always right on time. Our prayers initiate the most glorious opportunities for change; our only task is to let go of trying to control or define the "glorious" part. All we need is trust.

There is no easy way out of life; if you choose to go to sleep and ignore life and love, then you will find nothing but disappointment and regret in your afterlife. I have always found it ironic that the people who have really lived and loved life have an easier time dying that those who have lived in fear and bitterness and never enjoyed their time here. You would think that the people who love it here would have the hardest time letting go, but usually that's not the case. It is easier to leave a place when you know you have done your best and have a sense of "completeness" about it. A good life comes from the roots of good behavior. It does not come from envy or jealousy, or from a sense of resentment that you aren't getting what you think you deserve or want out of life.

If you want to be loved, be willing to love. Find out for yourself what it truly means to love well and freely, then take the risk. If you want to know if you are loved by another, ask yourself if you feel loved, and notice the behavior patterns. Love is shown, felt, and visible in subtle yet powerful ways. Love can be told, but if there is no action to back up the words, love has no vehicle. Words without love bounce off us and go out in the universe to be stored with the rest of our pretty words. Open all your senses to love. Pray that your heart will be open and you will be able to love, and then love again. Then go out and love some more!

## Opening to Love

• Each day in prayer, ask yourself the ultimate question: "How well have I loved?" Allow your answer to shape the way you treat yourself and others on a daily basis.

• In your prayers, ask to find the heart to behave lovingly and compassionately. Listen to the inspiration of God's voice telling you how to open to love.

• Be honest with yourself when you don't feel loving, and go within to explore the reasons. Allow chemistry to change when it needs to. Honest behavior requires an honest look at our feelings. Think of what blocks your love, and then ask God to remove the blocks. Is it that you cannot forgive a wrong done to you? Have you been too damaged by "love" to go out and love some more? If so, let yourself examine if it was truly love that damaged you; I doubt it. Again, pray for God's healing so you can open your heart to love.

• When you feel like you are "in love," remember to let some air come in so you don't suffocate. Remember that being "in love" may have little to do with the true willingness to love. Through your prayers, you can ask for the help of God in transforming attraction into the true love of affection, tenderness, and caring.

• Contemplate these wise words as you pray:

Friend, hope for the truth
while you are alive.
Jump into experience
while you are alive!
What you call "salvation"
belongs to the time before death.
If you don't break your ropes
while you are alive,
do you think ghosts will do it after?
The idea that the soul will join with the ecstatic
just because the body is rotten—
that is all fantasy.
What is found now is found then.
If you find nothing now,
you will simply end up with an
empty apartment in the City of Death.
If you make love with the Divine now,
in the next life
you will have the face of satisfied desire.

—Kabir

• I've always found Mother Teresa particularly inspiring with regard to compassion. Contemplate this quote of hers: "... it is in pardoning that we are pardoned....

"We shall always keep in mind that our community is not composed of those who are already saints, but of those who are trying to become saints. Therefore we shall be extremely patient with each other's faults and failures.

"None of us has the right to condemn anyone. Even though we see some people doing something bad, we don't know why they are doing it. Jesus invites us not to pass judgment. Maybe we are the ones who have helped make them what they are. We need to realize that they are our brothers and sisters. The leper, that drunkard, and the sick person is our brother because he too has been created for a greater love. This is something that we should never forget. Jesus Christ identifies himself with them and says, 'Whatever you did to the least of my brethren, you did it to me.' That leper, that alcoholic, and that beggar is my brother. Perhaps it is because we haven't given them our understanding and love that they find themselves on the street without love and care."

# The Alchemy of Being Human

## *The Experience of Reverence*

*I am done with great things and big plans,*
*great institutions and big success.*
*I am for those tiny, invisible, loving human forces*
*that work from individual to individual,*
*creeping through the crannies of the world*
*like so many rootlets, or like the capillary*
*oozing of water, which, if given time*
*will rend the hardest monuments of pride.*

— William James

*T*here is an ancient Chinese curse: "May you live in interesting times." We *are* living in interesting times. Are we cursed, or are we blessed? It is up to each of us to decide. At any rate, I think we need some urgent help using our time here, so that we can evolve instead of sleep-walking our way through life. The future of Mother Earth rests in the hands of moment-to-moment decisions by

God, and we are co-creating the outcome. Every action we take and each thought we ponder has an effect on the big picture. It is time to get back to basics. It is not a time to become more superstitious or afraid. It is a time to truly understand that *there is no power greater than God, and with God all things are possible.* No matter how crazy things get, no matter how many tragedies we see, God is in charge, and each of us has a guardian angel who ushers us forward in life, and in death. There is a simple thread of love that unites all life. When we second-guess God or project our own versions of tragedies upon life, we invite fear instead of trust. Prayer encourages us to trust. When we join in with God, we create a powerful synergy, alchemically changing the planet.

You chose to be here now in these interesting times. You may feel as if this was a crazy decision, but think of how brave you are. Think of that courageous spirit inside of you that came here to help God. Think about the gifts that allow you to transmit love out into the world. Some of these gifts are yet to be discovered, but they are with you now, and now is the time to find them. You are here to create stories of love, to connect deeply to others, to share love, to help the angels, to understand that death is not a punishment and not an end to love. The angels are always waiting to help you in each moment to wake up and love deeply. Loving is not easy, but anything worth having takes a bit of labor pain. Birth is painful and joyful, too. With the angels as our midwives, we are born into greatness and surrounded by miracles.

Miracles abound, angels exist, and there is proof of the powerful energy of God around us at all times; all we need to do is open our eyes, mind, and heart. We see the proof of God's power in the Qi Gong masters, who can hurl a person across the room by standing very still and pouring Qi energy out of their fingers. We get a sense of deep knowing each time we hear of the angels changing someone's life. The Twelve Step programs offer miracles daily. God is not a taboo word anymore. Prayer is powerful medicine. The tools are available, and we possess most of the ones we need to evolve. Are we using the tools, or are they sitting around collecting rust? You can have all the tools and materials you need to build a house, but nothing happens unless you pick up the tools and start using them. Make prayer one of the tools you reach for in your everyday life, and you will be blessed in ways that will deepen your reverence for living.

Have you ever really thought about the scope of being human? Have you truly pondered the full spectrum of all the colorful aspects to our beingness? Have you contemplated our human instincts, our beauty, the magic that is infused in our cells, the sacred nature of our fragile psyches, how we actually got here? Much of the time, it can seem pretty absurd to be a human. Many people have lost faith in the human spirit, because the human spirit can turn on itself in ways we cannot comprehend.

We are faced with a great challenge if we choose to pursue a sense of well-being and happiness. The question comes to us: How can I be happy when everyone seems to be suffering so much, when most of the world is starving and killing one another? Well, that is a valid question, but the fact is that the human spirit is striving to evolve, regardless of the circumstances and the judgments we lay upon it. Perhaps attaining our own happiness will imprint the soul of the world more deeply than anything else we could do.

This truth is the most serious aspect of alchemy: We are really here to evolve and become better, maybe only an inch better, but if we personally accomplish turning even one speck of our lead into gold, the world does become a better place. Now, the problem is that it is difficult to evolve if we do not have a sense of happiness in our soul, and happiness seems so elusive. The cosmic joke is that happiness is not really elusive; it is right inside of us. If we integrate prayer into our lives and allow ourselves a sense of gratitude, even for the smallest blessings, we will give that happiness room to flourish in our soul. True happiness is a state of God, and it comes without reason, without rhyme; it just is, and you know it by the feeling in your heart. When happiness is a regular visitor in our lives, it doesn't matter what we do—we are creating alchemy for the world's soul. Our little human spirit can accomplish amazing things, and often we don't even realize the magnitude of our effect on the world.

If you don't understand all of this now, start to pray for happiness anyway, and don't give up on your prayers. Don't try to answer your own prayers either. Let God and the angels take care of that; after all, they are the experts. What is an answered prayer anyway? Sometimes prayers are answered immediately. I have seen miraculous changes almost instantly after praying. Other times I don't recognize the answer until long after the fact. Most of the time, I simply need to keep renewing my trust and faith that God will answer my prayers, and then I get an understanding that the big picture is in process and our prayers are important ingredients in this big mix.

There are many things that encourage happiness. Everything I have talked about in this book encourages happiness. It is up to you to accept happiness. This is a monumental challenge, but you can master it. Remember to keep your sense of humor and your ability to have a good laugh. Go within and know your own beauty. Take the life you have been given and honor it. Have reverence for who you are right now. Cultivate reverence for all life. Do this in your own creative way. Use your own creativity to honor God. And, always remember that prayer is really the road to freedom. Trust yourself and begin to pray, and you will know how to live reverently.

### Discovering Reverence

• Ask yourself how would you pray each day if God spoke to you and told you that your main reason for being was to have fun and enjoy life. Ask yourself how you would pray if you saw God in every human face.

• Allow each spark of life to fill you with deep reverence and gratitude, and the sense that being human is glorious. The angels have blessed you with true lightness of being. Allow yourself to be truly happy without reason.

# The Alchemy of Our Ancestors

*Prayers, Psalms, and Verses That Inspire*

*From the mysterious regions*
*of our spiritual ancestors*
*come blessings subtle and profound.*
—S. Melikan

*D*o you know how your ancestors prayed? Do you know anything about your ancestors? One thing missing for many of us is the conscious awareness of the presence of our ancestors in our daily lives. I say "conscious awareness" because, recognized or not, they are with us. What spiritual heritage have they left us with? How do we go about evolving the patterns set forth in our DNA? What kind of prayers did they offer up to God?

There are many prayers that we grew up with or have heard and said over and over throughout our lives. Prayers that get passed down to us contain powerful words that we may not have looked at closely. Perhaps they have become automatic, and it is time to tune in and sense the true meaning behind the familiar words. I am including a few prayers from my ancestors in this book; because my main spiritual imprint is Christian, these are Christian prayers, but the true nature of any religion is universal, so I hope you will find they speak to you whatever your spiritual background. Look into the traditions from your own religious ancestry, and see them with new eyes. You may have ancestors from a variety of traditions. Start your own personal prayer collection encompassing prayers from a range of different religious traditions. Think about what these prayers mean, who wrote them, and what they tell you about the essence of prayer.

### Amen

I was taught to end each prayer I said with the words "In Christ's name, Amen." For years I said this without really thinking about what it meant. Now I understand that when I say these words I am agreeing to the highest principle of the Christ Consciousness; I am boosting the strength of my prayer by agreeing with Christ. *Amen* means to assent, to express agreement, and to consent.

### The Lord's Prayer

The Lord's Prayer is a prayer that is said around the world countless times a day. Here I give the version from the Amplified Bible. Jesus taught his followers to use this prayer, and he said: "Your Father knows what you need before you ask Him. Pray therefore like this."

### The Lord's Prayer

Our Father who is in heaven, hallowed [kept holy]
    be Your name.
Your kingdom come, Your will be done, on earth
    as it is in heaven.
Give us this day our daily bread,
And forgive us our debts, as we also have forgiven
    [let go of and given up resentment against]
    our debtors.
And lead [bring] us not into temptation, but
    deliver us from the evil one. For Yours is the
    kingdom and the power and the glory forever.
    Amen.

Matthew 6:8–13

### Divine Mother Energy

The quintessence of reverence and compassion is the Divine Feminine, the Divine Mother, the feminine face of God, which says, "Thou mayest" rather than "Thou shalt." When you want to be mothered, to feel the true essence of a love that has no conditions, no requirements, call upon the Divine Mother in heaven. The following prayers to the Blessed Virgin Mary have been used by countless people in times of severe danger, and numerous miracles have ensued.

> Hail, Mary, full of grace, the Lord is with thee.
> Blessed are thou among women, and blessed is the
>     fruit of thy womb, Jesus.
> Holy Mary, Mother of God, pray for us sinners
>     now and at the hour of our death.

> Hail, holy Queen, Mother of Mercy,
> Our life, our sweetness, and our hope.
> To you do we cry, poor banished children of Eve.
> To you do we send up our sighs,
> Mourning and weeping in this vale of tears.
> Turn, then, O most gracious Advocate,
> Your eyes of mercy toward us.
> And after this, our exile,
> Show unto us the blessed Fruit of your womb,
>     Jesus.
> O clement, O loving, O sweet Virgin Mary!

### Guardian Angel Prayer

I have treasured this prayer to my guardian angel ever since I learned it as a child.

Angel of God, my guardian dear,
To whom God's love commits me here;
Ever this day and night, be at my side,
To light and guard, to rule and guide.


### The Prayer of Saint Francis of Assisi

This prayer of Saint Francis speaks to the heart of the
alchemical power of prayer.


Lord, make me an instrument of your peace.
Where there is hatred, let me sow love.
Where there is injury, pardon;
Where there is doubt, faith;
Where there is despair, hope;
Where there is darkness, light;
Where there is sadness, joy.


O divine Master, Grant that I may not so much
    seek
To be consoled, as to console,
To be understood, as to understand,
To be loved, as to love,
For it is in giving that we receive;
It is in pardoning that we are pardoned;
It is in dying that we are born to eternal life.

### Saint Teresa of Avila's Bookmark

This simple prayer of Saint Teresa offers supplications to our soul. It is deeply comforting.

Let nothing disturb you,
Let nothing frighten you:
Everything passes away
Except God;
And God alone suffices.

### Psalms

A psalm is a "song" of praise to the Lord. Psalms have great power and can be used as part of a daily prayer ritual, for nothing can restore balance like tapping into the ancient laws of God. I often read the Ninety-First Psalm at angel gatherings, and one time a woman came up afterward and shared a beautiful story about this psalm. She had come to a very difficult place in her life, and was suffering deep depression, so deep that she was thinking about suicide. One day she reached out to her father and told him how depressed she was. He let her know he understood what she was going through and told her to promise him that before she did anything drastic she would read the Ninety-First Psalm every day for a month. This had helped him in a similar time. She did so, and said that it changed her life miraculously — this is truly the experience of the alchemy of prayer! The Twenty-Third Psalm has also served as an alchemical prayer for many across the centuries.

### PSALM 91 (AMPLIFIED BIBLE)

1 He who dwells in the secret place of the Most High shall remain stable and fixed under the shadow of the Almighty [Whose power no foe can withstand].

2 I will say of the Lord, He is my refuge and my fortress, my God, on Him I lean and rely, and in Him I [confidently] trust!

3 For [then] He will deliver you from the snare of the fowler and from the deadly pestilence. [Then]

4 He will cover you with His pinions, and under His wings shall you trust and find refuge; His truth and His faithfulness are a shield and a buckler. [Then]

5 You shall not be afraid of the terror of the night, nor of the arrow [the evil plots and slanders of the wicked] that flies by day,

6 Nor of the pestilence that stalks in darkness, nor of the destruction and sudden death that surprise and lay waste at noonday. [Then]

7 A thousand may fall at your side, and ten

thousand at your right hand, but it shall not come near you.

8 Only a spectator shall you be [yourself inaccessible in the secret place of the Most High] as you witness the reward of the wicked.

9 Because you have made the Lord your refuge, and the Most High your dwelling place, [Verses 1, 14]

10 There shall no evil befall you, nor any plague or calamity come near your tent.

11 For He will give His angels [especial] charge over you, to accompany and defend and preserve you in all your ways [of obedience and service].

12 They shall bear you up on their hands, lest you dash your foot against a stone. [Luke 4:10, 11; Heb. 1:14]

13 You shall tread upon the lion and adder, the young lion and the serpent shall you trample under foot. [Luke 10:19]

14 Because he has set his love upon Me, therefore will I deliver him; I will set him on high, because he knows and understands My name [has a personal knowledge of My mercy, love and kindness; trusts and relies on Me, knowing I will never forsake him, no, never].

15 He shall call upon Me, and I will answer him;
I will be with him in trouble, I will deliver
him and honor him.

16 With long life will I satisfy him, and show him
My salvation.

PSALM 23 (AMPLIFIED BIBLE)

1 The Lord is my shepherd [to feed, guide and
shield me]; I shall not lack.

2 He makes me lie down in [fresh, tender] green
pastures; He leads me beside the still and restful waters. [Rev. 7:17]

3 He refreshes and restores my life — my self; He
leads me in the paths of righteousness [upright-
ness and right standing with Him — not for
my earning it, but] for His name's sake.

4 Yes, though I walk through the [deep, sunless]
valley of the shadow of death, I will fear or
dread no evil; for You are with me; Your rod
[to protect] and Your staff [to guide], they
comfort me.

5 You prepare a table before me in the presence of
my enemies; You anoint my head with oil; my
[brimming] cup runs over.

6 Surely or only goodness, mercy and unfailing
love shall follow me all the days of my life;

and through the length of days the house of
the Lord [and his presence] shall be my
dwelling place.

### Building Your Personal Prayer Collection

• Ask older relatives to share with you prayers they
remember from their youth. This is a beautiful way to
connect with your ancestral spiritual tradition.

• Share your favorite prayers with your friends, and
ask them to do the same.

• The following books offer a wealth of prayers from
various traditions:

Appleton, George. *The Oxford Book of Prayer.* New York: Oxford
    University Press, 1985.
Easwaran, Eknath. *God Makes the Rivers to Flow: Selections From
    the Sacred Literature of the World.* Tomales, CA: Nilgiri Press,
    1991.
Penington, M. Basil. *Pocket Book of Prayers,* selected and intro-
    duced by M. Basil Penington. New York: Image Books,
    1986.
Roberts, Elizabeth, and Elias Amidon. *Earth Prayers From
    Around the World: 365 Prayers, Poems, and Invocations for Honoring
    the Earth.* San Francisco: HarperSanFrancisco, 1991.

• Write down the prayers that are meaningful to you
in a special prayer book, a treasure to inspire you for many
years to come.

# Acknowledgments

Dear God,

I thank you for the opportunity to write this book and share my love for the alchemical gift of prayer. Thank you for all the times I have witnessed great changes and examples of your love through prayer.

Thank you for my friends and family; the greatest gift I have in this life is their love which I carry in my heart.

Thank you for my two close friends/sisters and fellow writers who helped me tremendously with this book: Shannon Melikan and Jai Italiaander. They took a special interest in this book and helped with the research and development of ideas.

Thank you for the publishing team at H J Kramer Inc. Hal and Linda Kramer are examples of greatness in publishing. When I write a book with Linda's assistance, I am actually living a book. She allows for alchemy and spiritual growth to take place, and never rushes the creative process. Thank you for the blessing of having Nancy

Grimley Carleton as my editor; her integrity, kindness, and talent allow me to venture off in directions where I might not go otherwise because I know she will be there to sculpt the ideas like an artist. Thank you for the consistent support of Jan Phillips and Mick Laugs, who make sure the message gets out into the world.

Thank you for the loving support of my sister friends and fellow writers: K. Martin-Kuri, Holly Phillips, Rochelle Duffy, and Mary Beth Crain. Thank you for the insight and wisdom of my longtime comrade, Mark Neely.

Thank you for the special love and feeling of completeness that Joe Kelly Jackson has brought to my life.

Thank you, God, for the blessings in my life of true friends and a loving family, for by their love my life is rich in humor, meaningful experiences, and great teachers. I pray that every human on Earth may experience deep love and caring, for nothing creates alchemy more naturally than a true moment of compassion from a fellow human.

Thank you, God, from my heart and soul, spirit and mind, body and life force, for all the people I have never met, but who have blessed my life in so many ways.

Dearest God, may your blessings be accepted by all who read this book.

In Christ's name, Amen.

— Terry Lynn Taylor

## The Inner Light Series

The Inner Light Series is a collection of spiritual works that strive to inspire and illuminate the quest of a new generation of seekers. While the wisdom these books contain is classic, the language and metaphor through which it is expressed are contemporary and accessible to a wide and growing audience. We hope these books will become treasured companions on your unfolding journey of spirit.

### *Titles in the Series*

*The Laws of Spirit* by Dan Millman
*The Alchemy of Prayer* by Terry Lynn Taylor
*In Search of Balance* by John Robbins and Ann Mortifee